THE MICHAELS

Conversations During Difficult Times

Part One of The Michaels

Richard Nelson

BROADWAY PLAY PUBLISHING INC
New York
www.broadwayplaypublishing.com
info@broadwayplaypublishing.com

THE MICHAELS
© Copyright 2021 Richard Nelson

All rights reserved. This work is fully protected under the copyright laws of the United States of America. No part of this publication may be photocopied, reproduced, stored in a retrieval system, or transmitted, in any form or by any means, electronic, mechanical, recording, or otherwise, without the prior permission of the publisher. Additional copies of this play are available from the publisher.

Written permission is required for live performance of any sort. This includes readings, cuttings, scenes, and excerpts. For amateur and stock performances, please contact Broadway Play Publishing Inc. For all other rights please contact Patrick Herold I C M (U S A), Rose Cobbe United Agents (U K).

First edition: October 2021
I S B N: 978-0-88145-914-2

Book design: Marie Donovan
Page make-up: Adobe InDesign
Typeface: Palatino

THE MICHAELS was first produced by The Public Theater (Oskar Eustis, Artistic Director; Patrick Willingham, Executive Director), opening on 27 October 2019. The cast and creative contributors were:

ROSE MICHAEL..Brenda Wehle
DAVID MICHAEL..Jay O Sanders
SALLY MICHAEL...Rita Wolf
LUCY MICHAEL.................................... Charlotte Bydwell
IRENIE WALKER..Haviland Morris
MAY SMITH .... Matilda Sakamoto
KATE HARRIS .... Maryann Plunkett

Director.. Richard Nelson
Scenic Designer .... Jason Ardizzone-West
Co-Costume Designer..................................... Susan Hilferty
Co-Costume Designer..Mark Koss
Lighting Designer..Jennifer Tipton
Sound Designer .... Scott Lehrer
Dances based on original choreography by..... Dan Wagoner
Dance Coach ....Sara Rudner
Choreography Consultant............................Gwyneth Jones
Production Stage Manager ....Theresa Flanagan
Line Producer... Audrey Frischman
Company Manager ....Rebecca Sherman
Production Manager... Jeff Harris

CHARACTERS

ROSE MICHAEL, 66 [*A semi-retired choreographer, former artistic director of The Rose Michael Dance Company.*]

DAVID MICHAEL, 67, ROSE's *ex-husband. [Arts manager and producer; former manager of* ROSE's *company.]*

LUCY MICHAEL, 31, ROSE *and* DAVID's *daughter. [A dancer, choreographer with her own pick-up company. Lives in Washington Heights.]*

SALLY MICHAEL, 60, DAVID's *wife, and former principal dancer with* ROSE's *company. [Now part-time teacher.]*

IRENIE WALKER, *late 50s, former principal dancer with* ROSE's *company. [Now an administrator at Gibney Studios downtown. Lives in Manhattan.]*

MAY (MARY JANE) SMITH, 20s, ROSE's *niece (Her sister's daughter). [Dancer. Lives in Brooklyn.]*

KATE HARRIS, 66, [*Retired history teacher at Rhinebeck High School.*]

SETTING

Rose's *home; Rhinebeck, New York; which* The New York Times *once called "The town that time forgot".*

A small farmhouse near Long Pond, about a fifteen-minute drive from Rhinebeck Village. One of two farmhouses, which are set back together from Long Pond Road and share the same unpaved driveway.

Kitchen area.

Time: Sunday, October 27, 2019. 6 P M to approximately 9 P M.

NOTE ON THE DANCES

The original production of THE MICHAELS incorporated and adapted dances made in the 1980s and 1990s by the choreographer Dan Wagoner for his company The Dan Wagoner Dancers. For subsequent productions, other, appropriate, dances may be substituted.

NOTE ON MUSIC

For performance of copyrighted songs, arrangements or recordings referenced in this play, permission of the copyright owner(s) must be obtained.

AUTHOR'S NOTE

I use a single quotation mark to notate when the character is paraphrasing, and double quotation marks when the character is actually reading from a source.

Art is always, ceaselessly, occupied with two things. It constantly reflects on death and thereby creates life.
—Boris Pasternak, *Doctor Zhivago*

for Cynthia

(Furniture: piled on top of each other: chairs and benches, stool, worktable, dinner table, smaller table, a stove, sink, cabinet.)

(In the dark, Katie Herzig's **Best Day of Your Life** *plays through the main speakers.)*

*(*KATE *enters, then the others, with props, to set the furniture, and arrange and create* ROSE MICHAEL's *kitchen.)*

(The refrigerator is unseen and just 'off' in the 'pantry/ mudroom'.)

(Two entrances: the first from the back yard and lake, and pantry/ mudroom; the second from the rest of the house: front door and porch, living room, and upstairs, where there is the only bathroom.)

1.
The World Backstage.

(6 P M)

(Timer ticks on the stove. ROSE, DAVID *and* KATE. *A soup is cooking on the stove. A baguette is in the oven.* KATE *and* ROSE *make themselves a cup of tea.* DAVID *is in the middle of a story:)*

DAVID: You hear the ushers telling people to 'turn off your phones'. There's some music playing. Over here an actor's stretching in the dark; over there's another— her eyes are closed.

KATE: *(To* ROSE*)* You lived all this.

DAVID: All around you is just stuff: with taped labels: 'large pot', 'water pitcher.' 'Scene 5 box'. Lines of white tape on the floor: where you have to stand behind so you can't be seen by the audience. Someone's going like this... *(Pats his pants pocket)*

KATE: Why?

DAVID: —she's making sure she has her prop cigarettes. Another for his prop glasses. None of this the audience ever even knows about. Or thinks about. What's just behind... Just off. Before the play begins. The stage manager is handing out what to bring on. And I find myself walking onstage and the lights are coming up...

KATE: Oh my God!

ROSE: No understudies?

DAVID: We can't afford that, Rose.

KATE: What's happened to the actor whose part you played?

DAVID: I think he was just dehydrated. The hospital released him after like three hours.

KATE: Oh good.

DAVID: I was the right age. I was there. I held the script. The character mostly just sits in a chair. We would have had to cancel. I'd have lost a lot of money.

KATE: You never had to do this before?

DAVID: Never. All these years, Kate. I don't even hang around backstage, certainly not just before a play. Actors don't want that.

ROSE: Neither do dancers. We never wanted David backstage.

KATE: Why is that?

ROSE: *(To* DAVID*)* Explain it to her.

DAVID: It's their space, Kate. Actors, dancers…not the producer's… *(Himself)*. They even have rules about it. The point I'm trying to make is that I felt I'd been invited into a very solemn, almost spiritual, almost mystical world.

KATE: Backstage in a theater?

DAVID: *(Over this)* That I hadn't expected after all these years. Hadn't really thought about. It was neat… That's all. All I'm saying. *(To* ROSE*)* Am I being pretentious?

ROSE: *(To* KATE*)* When I used to wait in the wings with the other dancers, before going on, I always had this habit, to pull up my straps on my whatever I was wearing.

KATE: Why?

ROSE: I never knew I did that, until someone just pointed it out. I think Sally pointed it out.

DAVID: A ritual. Like crossing yourself.

ROSE: That's way too much, David. That's pretentious. *(To* KATE*)* I'd adjust the blouse or shirt or dress or— and go… Most of the time I was thinking— 'Rose, don't fall down.'

KATE: That's funny.

ROSE: Your actors were probably just thinking: 'where are we going to have dinner tonight?'

*(*KATE *wipes her hands and stands.)*

KATE: By the way, did you get lunch?

DAVID: They give you like a bag this big *(Very small)* of pretzels now.

KATE: I'll bet you were good. In that play… *(She heads off—to the refrigerator.)*

DAVID: *(Calls)* I wasn't. But thank you. *(To* ROSE*)* I got through it. No one left... My stage manager found me at intermission and told me to 'speak up, no one can hear you'.

ROSE: I don't think you were that bad.

DAVID: How do you know? You weren't there.

ROSE: Your stage manager filmed some of it. She sent it to me.

DAVID: What??

ROSE: On her phone. And she sent it to me. Just to me.

DAVID: What are you talking about?

ROSE: *(Over this)* Come on, David. Only to me and to your wife...

DAVID: Sally didn't say...

ROSE: And—to Lucy.

DAVID: Are you kidding?

ROSE: *(Continues)* And I've only sent it to my sister. You are very hard to hear, David.

DAVID: You're kidding.

ROSE: I did not send it to your brother. I don't know how he got it. Maybe Lucy.

(KATE *returns with a plate of cheeses.*)

ROSE: I haven't even shown Kate. *(Explains to* KATE*)* David's movie...

KATE: Not yet. She's promised.

DAVID: Kate, this is what our marriage was like.

ROSE: It was.

(SALLY *enters.*)

SALLY: Rose...

(IRENIE *is right behind her:)*

IRENIE: My train was late, Rose.

ROSE: That's Amtrak... We didn't hear you drive up. Irenie...

(They hug.)

IRENIE: The train was empty.

ROSE: Sunday, going north. Who does that? Everyone's going the other way.

IRENIE: It's a beautiful ride. Even in the rain.

ROSE: It is. Meet Kate. Kate, Irenie. Irenie, Kate.

IRENIE: *(Shaking hands)* How do you do, Kate. Rose has told me so much about you.

KATE: And she talks often about you too. Welcome to Rhinebeck.

IRENIE: It's wonderful to be in the country.

DAVID: Irenie...

IRENIE: David. Sally said you just got back too. Michigan. Touring a show?

DAVID: Ann Arbor.

IRENIE: *(Over this)* We could have come up together.

SALLY: He flew into Albany.

DAVID: Parking's cheap.

SALLY: David, Irenie, her bag's in the car.

ROSE: It's probably huge. It always was.

IRENIE: I'm staying a week.

SALLY: You don't need five pairs of shoes in the country.

IRENIE: In case we go out.

KATE: Take an umbrella.

SALLY: I left one on the porch.

DAVID: Irenie's staying with us?

SALLY: *(Of course)* With us. *(To* IRENIE*)* In David's study. That all right?

IRENIE: Anything…

(DAVID *has gone.*)

ROSE: *(To* IRENIE*)* David was just telling us all about what he said it felt like to him last night.

KATE: Being backstage at his play…

IRENIE: Right.

ROSE: *(To* IRENIE*)* There's a video of David's—

IRENIE: Sally just played it for me in the car.

ROSE: 'The magic of it all.' Is that what he called it? I kept thinking, remember Sally, right before she went on…?

IRENIE: I remember.

SALLY: What?

IRENIE: You'd always make a funny weird face.

SALLY: To break the tension. Get everyone to relax.

ROSE: After a while it wasn't funny, Sally. Everyone knew you were going to do it. So it wasn't funny. It was tedious. I just remember telling myself… In the wings before going on…

IRENIE: I know.

ROSE: What?

IRENIE: Don't fall down. Don't fall down.

ROSE: Right. That's right.

IRENIE: Me too. Don't fall down… Smells good in here.

SALLY: Kate's cooking.

IRENIE: I knew it couldn't be Rose.

SALLY: *(A joke)* No!!

IRENIE: *(To* KATE*)* You know she never ever cooks.

KATE: *(Smiles)* I've guessed that.

ROSE: Don't scare her away.

KATE: *(To* IRENIE*)* You've had lunch? There's cheeses…

ROSE: *(To* IRENIE, *over this)* Exotic cheeses from our farmers' market.

KATE: All from Dutchess County. So not so exotic, Rose.

ROSE: We were there all morning.

SALLY: Good for you.

KATE: In the pouring rain. Dinner about eight. Okay?

IRENIE: *(To* KATE*)* Ask her daughter. What *she* was fed growing up…

KATE: *(A joke)* Oh I did!

SALLY: The girls will be back soon.

KATE: They're rehearsing.

IRENIE: Before I do anything, I need to use the bathroom. I hate the ones on that train. They scare me…

KATE: The noise they make.

IRENIE: *(About the bathroom)* I can't remember…

SALLY: Upstairs. There isn't one on this floor. I'll show you.

ROSE: I should have added one downstairs. I'm going to regret that.

(As ROSE *stands:)*

KATE: Where are you going?

ROSE: I'm going to show Irenie the bathroom.

KATE: Rose...

ROSE: I can show her. I do the stairs. I do them every day. And, Kate, I think I might want to take a nap...

IRENIE: We passed two buses full of people looking at leaves.

KATE: In the rain?

ROSE: The leaves are gone.

IRENIE: Not all of them.

(They are gone.)

SALLY: A nap? The girls will be back soon. Irenie just got here...

KATE: We spent too long at the farmer's market.

SALLY: What can I do? What do you need?

KATE: I left things in my car...

SALLY: What am I doing? I can get them. You went to the farmers' market?

KATE: Her idea. She's 'going to get out.' In the backseat... It's open... Mostly bottles—wine, beer, seltzer... Thank you... The bag's heavy...

SALLY: If I see my husband I'll get him to help...

KATE: Thank you, Sally. She's tired...

(SALLY goes.)

(KATE looks through her recipes.)

(Lights fade.)

2.
Kate.

(The same, a short time later. KATE still with her recipes.)

(IRENIE enters, a loud bell is rung off.)

IRENIE: Rose is taking her nap. What was that?

KATE: These two houses used to be part of a summer camp... 'The dinner bell.' David rings it to scare off deer. I guess there's deer.

IRENIE: The country...

KATE: Rose says that in the winter you can see their tracks—

(Timer goes off.)

(KATE will head for the stove.)

KATE: —they come right up to her porch.

IRENIE: Mind if I hang out in here?

KATE: Of course not. Why would I—? No. Sit. Sit down. Anywhere... Relax. It's the country.

IRENIE: I was just sitting on the train...

(SALLY enters with a grocery bag and a six-pack of beer.)

SALLY: The rain stopped.

IRENIE: *(Before* SALLY *can ask)* She's resting. In her bedroom.

SALLY: You just got here...

(As KATE *takes out the baguette from the oven:)*

SALLY: Look at that. It's beautiful... *(To* IRENIE*)* From scratch.

KATE: It's hot. It needs to cool...

SALLY: All this in the fridge...?

KATE: Just the beer. The other just set on the pantry floor... There's already wine and... In the fridge... That's extra...

(SALLY heads off.)

IRENIE: Could I get a glass of—?

KATE: Help yourself.

IRENIE: How long do you think she'll nap for?

KATE: It depends.

IRENIE: Upstairs. In the hallway, are those Alice's paintings?

KATE: Some are. I didn't know Alice.

IRENIE: When she retired Alice wanted to paint. I think one is of Rose. Looks like Rose…

KATE: It does…I know the one.

(SALLY *enters from the pantry.*)

SALLY: *(To* KATE*)* Her fridge is full. I've never seen Rose's fridge full before.

KATE: I've planned something for every night.

SALLY: What can I get now? What can we do? Let us help.

KATE: The quiche dough… It needs to be out of the fridge…

IRENIE: I could do that… Let us help. Sit down.

SALLY: Don't do too much…

KATE: *(Over this)* It's easier for me… You don't have to sit in here… Both of you. Rose has a living room—.

SALLY: And leave you alone to make our supper?

KATE: And there's the porch. *(She goes.)*

IRENIE: *(Calls)* We're going to help. *(To* SALLY*)* Should we go on the porch? She just went into her room. 'To lie down'. And closed the door.

SALLY: *(Has picked up the hot water bottle)* This is cold.

IRENIE: Will Rose want another?

SALLY: *(Shrugs)* I'll pour this out.

IRENIE: Kate seems really nice.

SALLY: David and I think so.

IRENIE: And good for Rose. And hopefully good for Kate. But who knows? Probably not... That was a stupid thing to say.

SALLY: You all right?

(SALLY *sits with* IRENIE.)

IRENIE: It is what it is. I'm fine. And you've gotten to know her? Kate.

SALLY: We live here.

IRENIE: I wish I could have gotten up sooner...

SALLY: We've had her and Rose to dinner. *(A list)* Gone out to Upstate together...

IRENIE: Kate lives in Rhinebeck.

SALLY: The village.

IRENIE: And she teaches? Lucy told me she'd been one of her teachers in high school.

SALLY: Just retired.

IRENIE: Lucy said. And that's been hard on Kate, retiring.

SALLY: You know they had these big plans to travel?

IRENIE: Travel where?

(KATE *returns with a plate of dough for the quiche.*)

SALLY: Kate even got a new passport. She'd let it expire.

KATE: I had.

IRENIE: Should we be checking on Rose?

KATE: She just wants to rest.

IRENIE: You were Lucy's teacher in high school.

KATE: I was. One of them.

IRENIE: Her history teacher?

KATE: History. And debate team coach. Homeroom.

SALLY: In ninth grade.

IRENIE: But you never met Alice.

KATE: No. Never met Alice.

IRENIE: I would have thought—. I don't have kids—but parent-teacher conferences, school events—debates…

SALLY: Alice left all that to Rose, Irenie. And to David when he was around. It just seemed simpler… So I can see why Kate and Alice never met.

IRENIE: Kate, so how did you two meet? You and Rose. Can I ask?

KATE: Why can't you ask?

(DAVID *returns.*)

DAVID: Three deer in the driveway. And the girls are back. Why are you all in here?

IRENIE: *(To* DAVID*)* Rose is taking a nap.

DAVID: You just got here…

SALLY: Kate is making us all sorts of things.

KATE: Everyone doesn't have to stay in here.

IRENIE: *(To* DAVID*)* I asked how Kate and Rose met.

KATE: It's a small town.

DAVID: You two met at the library book sale, didn't you? That's what Rose told us. *(To* IRENIE*)* That's real Rhinebeck…

KATE: Is it? Why?

DAVID: *(To* IRENIE*)* They have them in the basement of the library. Like every few months. Twenty cents a book or something… What can I do to help, Kate?

KATE: Why don't we have something to drink besides water? I brought everything. Wine? Beer? I made herbal ice tea. In the fridge…

DAVID: What does everyone want?

KATE: I'll have wine, thank you. Whatever you want.

SALLY: Ice tea?

IRENIE: I don't care…

(DAVID *heads off to the pantry.*)

KATE: *(Calls)* You'll have to open the wine. *(To* SALLY*)* So Rose told you how we met? *(She will sit with* SALLY *and* IRENIE.*)*

SALLY: She did…Irenie, Kate volunteers at the book sale. And Rose told me she went there looking for mysteries…

KATE: I didn't know that. She was looking for mysteries?

IRENIE: She was always reading mysteries on tour….

SALLY: They were on a table in a side room, where the Historical Society also meets. And where there are old books behind glass. Old maps. Kate was working in this room, right?

KATE: She told you all this?

SALLY: She did. And Rose started to look at the old books, and Kate asks if she's interested in old things. Kate's a member of the Historical Society.

KATE: I was a history teacher.

IRENIE: You've just retired. And you're okay with that?

KATE: I'm fine. I miss the kids.

SALLY: And she recognizes you. She said you looked vaguely familiar…

KATE: Did she?

IRENIE: Lucy's teacher...

KATE: *(Long ago)* From ninth grade.

SALLY: And you—talked. And talked. And talked. And you agree to meet a couple of days later for coffee at Bread Alone. When you are both free.

IRENIE: And that was that your first date?

KATE: Was it?

SALLY: Wasn't it?

KATE: I guess so...

(Off, a screen door slams.)

KATE: I hear the young ladies...

SALLY: And she's a cook. Rose said she didn't know this at first, it was just dumb luck. *(A joke)* That's lucky for us!

IRENIE: Alice always did the cooking.

KATE: I had guessed something like that.

(LUCY *and* MAY *enter from outside.)*

LUCY: You're in here?

SALLY: Lucy, May... One more boring old dancer to tell you how *'she* did it.' Just what you need.

LUCY: Irenie, you made it. Thank you. *(To* KATE*)* Where's Mom?

KATE: Taking a nap.

IRENIE: *(To* SALLY*)* And so you're the other boring old dancer?

MAY: You guys aren't boring, Sally.

SALLY: So I'm old, May. Is that what you're saying?

MAY: No, I didn't mean... That's not what I was saying.

LUCY: They tease, May. They tease… They've been teasing me all my life.

(DAVID *has returned with the wine.*)

DAVID: Kate's cooking. We're keeping Kate company. You okay?

LUCY: Dad, Mom's taking a nap?

DAVID: Sally, let's have wine… What the hell?

IRENIE: How are you, May? Nice to see you out of New York City.

MAY: Hi, Irenie. It's good to be here.

DAVID: *(Surprised)* You know Rose's niece.

SALLY: May takes class at Gibney, David.

MAY: Every Tuesday.

DAVID: So you know each other from Gibney.

IRENIE: *(To* MAY*)* You're taking from Melanie.

SALLY: *(To* KATE*)* The dance world is about this *(Very small)* big.

KATE: Rose is always saying that.

LUCY: Sally the leak's back. Let's bring mops tomorrow.

MAY: We wiped some of it up… But it's a leak…

SALLY: *(To* DAVID*)* Remind me.

LUCY: We're going to wash up.

SALLY: Don't wake your mother….

LUCY: Why doesn't she want to be down here with you guys?

KATE: She's just tired. We went to the farmer's market.

DAVID: She's just taking a nap.

LUCY: We're having dinner, right?

DAVID: What do you think we're doing?

SALLY: We're not doing anything.

LUCY: Mom should be down here.

KATE: *(To* LUCY*)* It's going to be a while. It's cooking...

(LUCY *and* MAY *head upstairs.*)

DAVID: Sally, is she coming tomorrow? Has she said?

SALLY: Rose? *(Shrugs)*

KATE: *(To* DAVID*)* The girls have been up here all week... Working really hard...

SALLY: *(To* DAVID*)* I'm not Rose. I try.

IRENIE: When does Lucy go to Europe?

DAVID: Not for a few months.

IRENIE: Where's your dance studio now? You had to move...

DAVID: *(Explains everything)* It's Rhinebeck.

SALLY: The little mall across from the Fairgrounds, by the laundromat.

DAVID: Hence the leak.

SALLY: You'll see tomorrow. There's a kids' karate school next door. We share a wall... What can we do, Kate? We're just sitting here.

IRENIE: *(Over this)* If we're going to stay in here...

KATE: It's a lot more comfortable in the living room....

SALLY: Come on...

KATE: You all don't have to stay in here...

DAVID: *(Obviously)* It's the kitchen...

(Lights fade.)

3.
The Retrospective

(The same a short time later.)

*(*DAVID, SALLY, IRENIE *and* KATE, *who continues to work the dough:)*

*(*LUCY *and* MAY *are returning:)*

DAVID: You didn't wake your mother? She'll come down…

LUCY: Her door was closed, Dad.

KATE: *(To* LUCY *and* MAY*)* You girls need anything?

LUCY: We're fine, Kate.

MAY: I'm good…

IRENIE: So who else is part of this?

DAVID: The performance?

IRENIE: The usuals?

DAVID: Some surprises. *(For example:)* Miranda.

IRENIE: Really? That's great.

DAVID: Good for them. I can show you the list.

IRENIE: *(Continues)* I ran into Miranda at Gibney a couple of months ago.

SALLY: *(To* KATE*)* Wonderful dancer. Choreographer. Rose's age.

DAVID: A little older. *(To* LUCY*)* You know her, Miranda.

LUCY: I do.

SALLY: You run into everybody there.

IRENIE: Miranda was super friendly…

SALLY: Was she.

IRENIE: We chatted by my desk. She came to ask could we turn down the air.

DAVID: She's teaching?

IRENIE: I think she was just visiting someone at Gibney. I hadn't seen her there before. Anyway we got talking. Over my desk there's the poster of Merce?

SALLY: I love that poster.

MAY: Me too.

IRENIE: *(Over this)* And she smiles. Why are you smiling, Miranda? When she was a girl; she grew up in Brooklyn, did you know that?

DAVID: No.

IRENIE: Her uncle had a loft in Manhattan, where all sorts of people rehearsed. Dan. Paul Taylor.

DAVID: Kate, we couldn't ever afford it.

IRENIE: She remembered being a little kid, being introduced to Merce, with those big bushy eyebrows, and she remembers thinking: 'oh my god, it's the devil!' She just wanted to talk. She seemed lonely.

SALLY: I haven't seen Miranda forever.

IRENIE: I don't think she spends a lot of time now around dancers. I think just being at Gibney…

SALLY: Brings up stuff… Sure. Churns up…

IRENIE: She then stood in the hallway watching a class through the window. I went up to her: 'Anything you need, Miranda? Drink of water? Cup of coffee?' I startled her. I think she didn't know who I was. We'd just been talking… This retrospective is a very good thing for her.

SALLY: As it is for Rose…

LUCY: And for us… *(Her and* MAY*)*

IRENIE: *(To* DAVID*)* You know I thought they were only going to do new stuff.

DAVID: The Lumberyard?

IRENIE: *(Continuing)* But that they're doing retrospectives—that's good, isn't it?

DAVID: I think they're doing what they do to get on the map.

SALLY: From the seventies and eighties.

IRENIE: The golden age, Kate.

KATE: Was it?

LUCY: They're also renting it all out for weddings and stuff.

DAVID: Anything to make a go of it. Bless them.

IRENIE: I haven't been.

DAVID: *(To* LUCY, *explains)* It's not in New York.

SALLY: *(Teasing)* It's 'far away' in Catskill.

KATE: Only women were chosen for this show? Is that right?

SALLY: The choreographers are all women. Yeh.

IRENIE: It's not really called a 'show.'

SALLY: It can be. Just women…

KATE: I don't know anything about dance.

IRENIE: *(To* KATE*)* You'll come tomorrow to watch the girls rehearse?

SALLY: She's coming.

KATE: *(Same time)* I'm coming. Can't wait…

LUCY: Irenie, the tapes are grainy. I'm warning you… There's stuff we can't figure out.

IRENIE: That's why I'm here… We'll look at them together tomorrow.

LUCY: We've been waiting.

SALLY: I've been here.

MAY: The dances are fun. And they're funny,

IRENIE: I know. I danced them.

(KATE *will butter the bottom of a glass pie plate and begin to shape in the quiche dough.*)

MAY: They don't let you do funny very much any more.

DAVID: No? Why?

LUCY: I don't know.

SALLY: Everything's very serious now. In the 'dance world'.

DAVID: It's a really small budget, Irenie. Like the old days…

LUCY: Mom keeps complaining that it won't show off her 'real range'.

IRENIE: But Rose hasn't seen anything, Sally said.

DAVID: No.

LUCY: Not yet. We've been rehearsing on our own. With Sally. Let me show you what they've sent out… It looks really nice. Kate, where did we put the—?

KATE: The brochure? I think with the mail…

(LUCY *will find a brochure with the mail.*)

SALLY: We've seen it.

DAVID: Sh-sh. I thought I heard her…

(*Pause. They listen.* LUCY *will hand* IRENIE *the brochure.*)

DAVID: No. You can hear everything in this house.

LUCY: I grew up here. I was a teenager here…

DAVID: They did a nice job with that… (*Brochure*)

IRENIE: *(Looking at the brochure)* Very nice. I know everybody...

SALLY: Me too.

LUCY: They're doing a whole exhibit in the Hudson Opera House.

IRENIE: About—?

SALLY: *(Obviously)* About the choreographers in the show. Rose gets an entire wall.

IRENIE: Fantastic. No one told me.

DAVID: *(Over this)* And display case. *(To* LUCY*)* Two, we think.

LUCY: We've asked. We're trying.

DAVID: Keep asking.

LUCY: Dad.

MAY: She's asked like five times, David.

DAVID: Quotes, photos. I think we'll project one of the old videos on a wall. That's our plan....

LUCY: One of the good ones where you can actually see what's happening.

IRENIE: So they get some context. Younger dancers especially have no context.

MAY: I don't agree.

LUCY: That's not really true, Irenie.

IRENIE: That's what I see every day at Gibney...

LUCY: And Dad—you don't even know about this—

DAVID: What don't I know?

LUCY: They're putting out a kind of journal... We just found out, didn't we, May?

MAY: Lucy got an e-mail out of the blue.

LUCY: *(To* MAY*)* It's in the drawer....? *(She will find a small notebook out of a drawer.)*

IRENIE: Rose should be over the moon. This *(The brochure)* is great.

LUCY: May keeps a notebook in here.

MAY: You never know when she'll talk.

LUCY: She talks in the kitchen.

DAVID: What's that?

LUCY: *(Over this)* For this journal, Dad. We've begun interviewing Mom.

MAY: Trying to.

LUCY: May and me.

IRENIE: On tape?

LUCY: She won't talk into a tape recorder, Irenie.

DAVID: *(To* SALLY*)* Why not?

MAY: She just won't.

*(*MAY *hands* LUCY *the notebook.)*

IRENIE: They should get it on tape. So we have your mother's voice.

MAY: So we've been writing things down.

LUCY: *(To* MAY*)* You do.

MAY: Sometimes Aunt Rose talks.

LUCY: And when she does... Here... Just from this week... *(Shows* DAVID*)*

IRENIE: All of that?

LUCY: *(About the notebook)* My favorite so far...

DAVID: *(To* LUCY*)* You read it to us...

LUCY: *(Reads)* You want me to? Okay... Here: "Yvonne. That's who we watched. She was the most articulate of any of us. Maybe sometimes so much so that it all got a bit too theoretical at times. But that mostly came later."

DAVID: I didn't know about…

SALLY: You've been away all week.

KATE: Yvonne?

DAVID: Rainer…

LUCY: *(Reads)* "At this time, there was still humor. And Yvonne and Trisha telling all they'd learned from Halprin. I'll get to that, girls. *My* time with Anna Halprin."

IRENIE: Rose spent time with Halprin? She's never talked about that. *(To* MAY*)* She was—.

MAY: I know who she is.

KATE: Who's…?

SALLY: A kind of guru. *(To* IRENIE*)* She's talked about that with me.

IRENIE: *(Over the end of this)* Not me. When?

DAVID: *(Over this)* Keep reading, Lucy…

LUCY: *(Reads)* "She led the way for me." *(Explains)* Yvonne. *(Read)* "How dance could be about human movements. Not artificial ones. How it's not a sport, with rules like that. 'Positions.' I can hear Yvonne say that word with such revulsion, spitting it out: 'positions.'"

IRENIE: Kate, she means ballet.

LUCY: *(Reading)* "So we began with: some basic simple actions. Like vacuuming. I made a dance around vacuuming."

KATE: Really?

DAVID: She did. Remember? She obviously wants to talk. You girls are getting her to talk.

LUCY: May asks most of the questions.

MAY: I do. I'm interested. I try.

LUCY: *(Reads)* "Another dance: sweeping—with a broom. Yvonne saying to us, 'A dance can be someone folding laundry. Everyday, pedestrian movements: walking, sitting, falling…'" That's when Mom stopped, and grabbed ahold of May's hand, May was taking the notes. To stop May writing. "Why are we talking about this?" She gets going… The mood strikes, I guess. And then… She just stops.

DAVID: May I see…?

(LUCY *gives* DAVID *the notebook.*)

SALLY: *(To* IRENIE*)* I ran into Yvonne Rainer.

IRENIE: Where?

SALLY: Kaatsbaan. *(To* DAVID*)* I told you. This summer. August.

IRENIE: What was she doing there?

SALLY: I guess she knew the dance company. Had friends… *(She will bring cheese and crackers to the table.)*

IRENIE: Did you talk to her?

SALLY: Yeh. I mean, she wouldn't know me. But I went up to her, during the intermission. She was alone, looking at the sculptures in the lobby. I introduced myself—you don't know me, but I was a principal with Rose Michael's company. And…

IRENIE: What?

SALLY: Irenie, she just lit up. And looked at me closely, and said, 'I think I recognize you, Sally.'

IRENIE: She remembered your name?

DAVID: She'd just introduced herself.

SALLY: She knew all about Alice.

DAVID: It's a small world.

SALLY: Asked if I ever saw Rose. I said we live next to each other just outside Rhinebeck. She asked how she was getting along without Alice...

IRENIE: She didn't ask anything else?

SALLY: No.

IRENIE: She doesn't know?

(SALLY *shrugs.*)

DAVID: *(Looking through the notebook)* Lucy and May are choosing photos. For the wall. You're still doing that?

LUCY: Most of them Mom doesn't even want to look at. She won't tell us who is who...

IRENIE: Maybe I can help.

LUCY: May got her talking once about...

IRENIE: About...?

MAY: I asked Aunt Rose about when she was a girl? You know, with my mother...

DAVID: She talked about that?

LUCY: This I thought was interesting, Dad.

MAY: She wouldn't let me write it down.

SALLY: Why not?

MAY: "For family only." She said she often wondered if the interest in 'normal boring movement' —her words—people just 'doing things', if it came out of growing up in the motel.

DAVID: I've never heard her say that.

LUCY: Me neither. And she asked May—.

MAY: She asked me if I felt anything like that too, having grown up in the same damn motel...

DAVID: She hates that motel.

SALLY: I know.

LUCY: *(Over this)* Explain it... What she said, May.

MAY: As a kid, she'd sit all day watching these strangers come and go. Just sit on the stairs, by the front desk, sip a coke, and watch... She said my mother would just stare at her, *(In a voice)* 'Rose what the hell are you doing?' That's her impression of my mother. It's pretty close. And Aunt Rose would say to her, 'I'm watching people.'

DAVID: *(To* MAY*)* Have you asked your Mom if she remembers doing that?

MAY: Not yet.

DAVID: Pina Bausch used to say the same thing. Her parents ran a hotel...

MAY: *(To* LUCY*)* Did you know that?

SALLY: I didn't know that.

LUCY: Sometimes right after dinner Mom will talk... She says she likes talking to May... In the kitchen.

DAVID: Here. *(Reads)* "Trisha came into the studio—

SALLY: Trisha Brown.

MAY: I know. I know.

DAVID: *(Continues)* "... Trisha Brown sat on the floor and spread her legs a hundred and eighty degrees, and then, put her *stomach* on the floor. I watched in awe, and said to myself, Jesus Christ, it's over. I can't do that."

(IRENIE *and* SALLY *smile.*)

DAVID: *(Reads)* "Trisha was always saying 'I always feel sorry for the parts of the stage that aren't used.'" Rose says, "I don't know why."

IRENIE: What does that mean?

DAVID: *(Reads)* Here: "Anna Halprin…"

LUCY: You never know when she's going to talk. Or what question she's going to answer.

SALLY: *(To* IRENIE, *proving her point)* Anna Halprin.

DAVID: *(Reads)* "… always told us to get the audience to identify not with the dancer, but the person. How does that person's body react when going uphill? Going downhill? What happens when that body is carrying many objects?" *(Turns a page. Reads)* "We danced on Anna's famous outdoor deck. I once asked her, what do we do if it rains? She said, 'The rain will run down our backs and out between the boards of the deck. It's just another part of the dance.'" *(Another paragraph. Reads:)* "One learned why to move rather than just learning movements."

LUCY: Read what's next, Dad. We asked Mom if we could make this the title of her whole display, her wall…

IRENIE: What did she say?

LUCY: She doesn't care.

MAY: She didn't answer.

DAVID: *(Reads)* "So this led me to ask myself, not 'how do people move,' but rather 'what moves people?'" Is that your title?

(LUCY *nods.)*

IRENIE: *(To* 'ROSE'*)* Rose you should have written a book.

DAVID: This *(Notebook)* could be a start.

SALLY: It really could.

IRENIE: You girls might like this.

LUCY: What?

IRENIE: I had a boyfriend. When I'd just hooked up with your Mom and Sally. I was a baby. He was a sculptor.

DAVID: The sculptor. Oh I remember him.

IRENIE: *(Over this)* And Rose thought maybe my new boyfriend would make sets for us for free, so she invites him to come along and watch us rehearse for an afternoon. I think this was at Dancer Players on 6th?

SALLY: How do you remember that?

DAVID: It was so cheap. I loved it.

SALLY: You get what you pay for.

IRENIE: My boyfriend comes along and watches as your mom—your aunt—led us through some 'improvisations of pedestrian movement.'

SALLY: *(Laughs)* I remember this.

LUCY: What?

MAY: *(Same time)* What?

IRENIE: She'd call out: 'jump', or 'fall', 'laugh', 'hug', 'disrobe'.

LUCY: *(To* MAY, *smiling)* Disrobe?

MAY: You'd take off your clothes?

DAVID: Don't get her started. Don't ask questions.

IRENIE: *(Over this)* We did this all afternoon. This was our dancing. So I'm walking home with my boyfriend and I ask him what he thought, what he liked best. He says, that for him, the best parts—were when we weren't dancing.

(Laughter)

SALLY: When Irenie first came to us...

DAVID: Lucy and May, what have you done?

LUCY: I didn't ask...

SALLY: *(Over this)* Be quiet.

IRENIE: What are you going to tell them?

SALLY: The truth. Irenie wanders in off the street. And the first thing she says, 'I went to Vassar.'

IRENIE: That wasn't the first thing—. *(To* LUCY*)* I'd heard of your mother and the work she was trying to do.

SALLY: *(Over this)* The very first thing. Completely stuck up. *(To* DAVID*)* Wasn't she?

DAVID: I don't know.

SALLY: Coward. *(Continues)* I introduced myself. 'Well I went to Queens High.' I think you were even wearing gloves.

IRENIE: That's a lie.

SALLY: Like three weeks later it comes out that she'd first tried classes at Martha Graham's but she couldn't hold her stomach in!

IRENIE: That's true. That is true.

KATE: I don't understand.

LUCY: Mom should be down here.

DAVID: I know.

SALLY: *(To* KATE*)* We were looser. Your stomach was your stomach, Kate.

LUCY: *(To* MAY*)* We should be interviewing them.

(KATE *will put the crust into the oven and set the timer.*)

DAVID: *(About* KATE*)* It's going in.

KATE: Just the crust. Eat some cheese.

SALLY: We're fine.

IRENIE: *(To* DAVID*)* The summer when you got that grant from, was it NYSCA? Is there still a NYSCA?

DAVID: Not really. Now we're into war stories.

LUCY: What happened?

DAVID: They had a rule we had to dance in some public space in *each* of the five boroughs. Manhattan was easy. The Bronx—

IRENIE: We danced in the botanical gardens. The guards kept shouting, stay on the path!

SALLY: Staten Island. The Ferry Waiting Room. We thought—.

DAVID: I didn't arrange that. I didn't produce this.

IRENIE: *(Over this)* We thought that there'd be a stage, or we'd at least be roped off.

DAVID: I did not organize this.

IRENIE: We were given a time for evening rush hour, to get the biggest crowd, we were told. But there is no stage, so we just mark out an area in chalk. And then a ferryboat arrives, and we start to dance—and the crowd just runs right through us. Like we were just in the way. Someone even stepped on Elaine's foot—.

(ROSE *enters from upstairs.*)

ROSE: You're laughing.

DAVID: Rose...

ROSE: What did I miss?

IRENIE: We're telling stories...

SALLY: Boring the girls...

IRENIE: I'm here a week. I'm sure we'll tell them again.

DAVID: And again.

LUCY: Get some rest, Mom?

ROSE: I couldn't sleep...

(Lights fade.)

4.
Rose.

(The same. A short time later.)

(ROSE has joined them at the table. KATE has stopped working. In the middle of a conversation:)

ROSE: I had a deal with them, Irenie. It was a goddamn commission. Where's the e-mail, Kate? Isn't it down here? You printed it out.

KATE: I printed what out?

LUCY: I did Mom.

DAVID: I think I left it on the porch, Lucy.

LUCY: I'll get it… *(She goes off.)*

KATE: I don't know anything about this, Rose. You haven't told me anything. What— 'commission'?

ROSE: *(To* DAVID*)* Explain it to her…

DAVID: *(To* KATE*)* Rose was asked to make a piece for a big dance company. They have a young studio company attached to them.

ROSE: This fucked up dance world.

DAVID: *(Continues)* And each year, Kate, this studio company does a program with the young dancers of the Royal Ballet in London.

KATE: London?

DAVID: And a choreographer is commissioned to make half a dance on the American kids, and the other half on the English kids, and then they all come together and perform the whole piece. A pretty big deal.

SALLY: This coming year that's going to be in England, Kate.

(LUCY has returned with the e-mail.)

ROSE: I was going to take you to London. It was going to be a surprise.

KATE: When were you going to do this?

IRENIE: *(Taking the e-mail)* Thanks. *(To* LUCY*)* When did Gareth send this?

LUCY: Yesterday, Irenie. I sent it to Dad last night.

(As IRENIE *reads the e-mail:)*

DAVID: *(To* ROSE*)* I'm going to call Gareth in the morning. I'm going to make sure you get paid. In full. You did have a deal.

SALLY: Two companies of dancers, two countries: the whole project would take a year, Kate.

KATE: A year?

SALLY: That's a long time…

IRENIE: It is.

KATE: Can I see that when you're done?

ROSE: When I told them that I was sick, I wasn't saying I couldn't do it.

SALLY: I know you didn't mean that.

ROSE: It's not what I was saying. I thought I was being responsible—in case I needed to rest for a day, or have doctors' appointments. I wasn't asking to be fired…

SALLY: I don't think anyone's firing you, Rose.

ROSE: Isn't that what he's just done?!

SALLY: Is it really?

*(*IRENIE *reading:)*

IRENIE: He's a good man. A friend.

ROSE: Which side are you on?

SALLY: There are no sides, Rose.

*(*KATE *will pick up the e-mail.)*

IRENIE: I read this as a friend who is worried about you. We've known Gareth for years. He's concerned. He wants to make sure you are taking care of yourself.

ROSE: What the fuck does that mean?! Read that!

IRENIE: I am.

DAVID: Lucy, May, you okay? You don't need to stay...

ROSE: They're fine.

LUCY: We'll stay, Dad.

ROSE: I had a deal.

IRENIE: I know.

ROSE: What do you think?

IRENIE: I don't know. But we are all concerned, aren't we?

ROSE: About what? What are you talking about?

IRENIE: You know.

ROSE: No, I don't know. What?

IRENIE: Like Gareth says, concerned that you're doing everything possible, Rose.

ROSE: You stand in my shoes for a little bit, and try to choose the best care from the choices I've got. And then figure out how to judge me.

LUCY: No one is judging you, Mom.

IRENIE: *(Same time)* Come on, Rose.

SALLY: No, of course not—. Gareth is just worried. He means well.

IRENIE: He says he hadn't heard from you for a while...

ROSE: I've been busy. *(To* IRENIE*)* He writes me all this in a goddamn e-mail.

DAVID: I agree. This should not have been an e-mail.

IRENIE: He says he's tried to call. You don't pick up.

DAVID: Then keep trying.

IRENIE: Sometimes silence speaks really loud. And so friends, real friends, start to worry. When there's—silence. Committing yourself to new work that will take you maybe—a whole year... Before going down that path...

ROSE: That's not for him to decide.

IRENIE: No. No.

ROSE: I'm going to live.

IRENIE: Of course you are.

ROSE: I watched Alice...

SALLY: We all did.

ROSE: She lived for almost *two* years. And she worked.

IRENIE: I don't think they're just trying to protect themselves, David.

DAVID: It's one way to read it.

ROSE: Ask him which poison would he have me take?

LUCY: Mom...

ROSE: What hell does he want me to put myself through? I'm doing everything I can...

IRENIE: That's great. And—what is that? Could you tell us?

ROSE: What is what?

IRENIE: Sally says you won't tell her what you're doing...

SALLY: We talk.

ROSE: I don't believe this. I have done nothing else for the past two months except try and get better! *(To* KATE*)* Haven't I? Kate, haven't I, tell them.

KATE: I don't know that.

ROSE: I research treatments, I call doctors, track down so-called immune therapy 'experts'. They tell me — find some kind of trial. I spend a lot of time doing this. I have talked with five major—*major*—oncology doctors. That takes time. And each one suggests a different medication.

DAVID: It's hard. I know.

ROSE: You try sorting through the piles of medical crap... With those insane drug names. And all those useless doctors who have no idea how to help me...

(Silence)

LUCY: Irenie, Gareth makes a suggestion...

IRENIE: I saw that. Rose, what about his suggestion here? We haven't talked about that. It seems to me to be an offer.

LUCY: That's how I read it.

ROSE: We talked about this, Lucy.

IRENIE: As a substitute for the commission: a solo piece for their new dance series.

SALLY: They do that up here at Kaastbaan.

LUCY: They do.

IRENIE: Then you could work from home.

LUCY: Kaastbaan's just down the road.

IRENIE: Sleep in your own bed, Rose. No travelling. Save your strength for the work. It's an interesting idea...

ROSE: 'Generous', you mean?

SALLY: Why do you say it like that?

IRENIE: What do you think? Have you had time to think about it? A solo piece...

ROSE: Solos are just masturbatory...

SALLY: Since when? You've done tons of them. I've danced them.

IRENIE: Me too.

LUCY: *(Over this)* We're right now doing two of your old ones, Mom.

MAY: We are.

DAVID: What they took away was a really big deal. Not a solo at Kaastbaan.

ROSE: Kate, I've been working on their commission for three months. Planning what to do... Three goddamn months.

KATE: That's a long time. I didn't know.

ROSE: I'd worked it all out. In here... *(Her head)* ...Kate, all my doctors—*all* of them—recognize my desire to work.

KATE: Do they? You haven't told me.

ROSE: All of them have urged me to keep working as much as I can. *(She takes the e-mail.)* Irenie, you know what this means...

IRENIE: What?

ROSE: Now all over New York they're chattering away like in high school: 'Rose is unable to properly take care of herself.'

IRENIE: *(Over this)* He says he writes in confidence, Rose. He says that right there.

ROSE: He's made sure that everyone, all of New York, knows to run in the other direction when they see me coming...

LUCY: That's not true, Mom. Please...

ROSE: Kate, you don't know the dance world.

KATE: I don't.

(ROSE *gets up.*)

KATE: What do you need? Rose?

ROSE: I'm not an invalid. Not yet, Kate. (*She goes off.*)

IRENIE: The dance world is not like that.

DAVID: Can be…

IRENIE: What is she doing? (*To* SALLY) Has she really seen all these doctors? I hadn't gotten that impression.

SALLY: Kate?

KATE: I don't know when she sees them…

IRENIE: Is she driving?

KATE: No.

(SALLY *looks off; thinks she hears* ROSE *coming back, but she isn't, then:*)

SALLY: (*To* IRENIE) Sometimes David and I have come over in the morning. (*To* KATE) Haven't we? (*To* IRENIE) This, more than once, and she's in a state, been up all night at the computer. As if she's going to solve everything that way by herself. It's a fucking mess. I don't think she even has one doctor who's in charge.

KATE: She doesn't. I've been living with this.

DAVID: One of the actors on my tour, his wife visited him this week. She's a gynecologist… So I asked. All I say is: 'Stage 4. Ovarian.' She shakes her head. I say, we don't think she's really doing much about it. Maybe even nothing. What if she's doing nothing? The actor's wife said, "Maybe that's what I'd do in her shoes…"

LUCY: No.

DAVID: You all right, Lucy?

LUCY: I'm fine…

(ROSE *returns with two beers.*)

ROSE: May, I brought you a beer. May and I like beer. Don't we?

MAY: *(Taking a beer)* We do, Aunt Rose. Thank you.

ROSE: May, you got that bottle opener?

(MAY *will open the beers.*)

ROSE: I have a growth, right here… *(Waist)* You can touch it if you want. *(To* IRENIE*)* Do you want to touch it?

IRENIE: Sure…

(ROSE *lets her touch it, as:*)

ROSE: I had to go and buy pants with a stretchy waist. I used tell Alice, if she ever saw me in pants with a stretchy waist, please shoot me. She said she would. I've asked Kate to do the same. This *(*KATE*)* coward refuses…

KATE: I do. I'm a coward.

ROSE: And May…

MAY: *(Surprised)* What, Aunt Rose?

ROSE: May, can you please tell your mother, my dear sweet sister, to stop worrying about me. She calls like every day now. Always at the wrong time. I go on the toilet—my sister calls. Every time. Every—goddamn time. *(To* KATE*)* Right? You've seen it.

KATE: It's true. It's amazing.

DAVID: She's always been like that.

ROSE: And what's there to say?

MAY: I'll tell her, Aunt Rose. She's asked me to come up and help her out for a while. I'll try and keep her off the phone. No more than—how's twice a week? How's that?

ROSE: And May, don't you get stuck up there in Utica with your Mom and that idiotic motel. It'll just make you bitter. Like your Mom.

MAY: I'll be careful, Aunt Rose.

(ROSE *folds up the e-mail, then:*)

ROSE: It was in two parts, Kate.

KATE: What was? What are you talking about?

ROSE: My dance for the kids. What I've been working on for months. It had to be... That was the rule. One part America, one part England. *(Then)* Part one, Irenie: a young woman with children and a husband. She's happy. Then one day Death appears. From a Greek play. He has come for her father-in-law. But he's not ready to die, he tells Death. Someone has to, because I'm here, Death replies. But no one will sacrifice himself for the old man. Until the young wife steps forward. Take me, and spare my father-in-law, she says. Or gestures. Dances. Everyone is shaken, everyone is sad, but they let her do it. *(Real questions)* Why? Better her than me? *(Then. Real question:)* Is that what people feel when they're around someone dying? Just curious. So with much crying—and dancing, Death carries the young woman away. *(Then)* Part Two: To this house comes an old family friend, Hercules. The same. He arrives with pals, they are drunk; they dance, carouse, totally unaware of what has just taken place. When told, Hercules immediately sobers up; charges away—dancing. Dives down into Hades—dancing; where he finds Death still carrying the young woman over his shoulder. He fights Death, frees her, brings her back to life and to her home. Now veiled, she stands in front of her guilty family; who are still deep in mourning. Hercules urges the husband—welcome this mysterious veiled woman into your home; the husband refuses, he is in too much pain, too much guilt; when Hercules unveils her. And something in the world seems to be set right again; when all had seemed lost, all are now reunited. All of the dancers from the first part, and all from the second, joyously dance together... But then at the very last moment, she walks out of the dance. She turns and watches the happy couples, who only a short while ago had been so relieved that it was not them that Death had taken away.... *(Then)* I've been planning it. *(Standing)* May, could I have one of your cigarettes, please?

(MAY *takes out a pack and takes out a cigarette to hand to* ROSE.)

ROSE: You smoke. Kids don't smoke anymore.

(*As* MAY *gives* ROSE *a cigarette:*)

ROSE: You have your lighter?

MAY: Matches, Aunt Rose...

(MAY *gives* ROSE *her matches.*)

(ROSE *heads off out the back.*)

IRENIE: Where is she going?

LUCY: Out the back. Probably going for a walk around the lake...

(No one knows what to say.)

DAVID: She was trying to turn everything, all that she's going through, into—something else. And they took that away.

(KATE *wipes her hands on her apron.*)

KATE: Excuse me...

(KATE *follows* ROSE *out.*)

DAVID: *(To* IRENIE*)* She's started smoking... Alice would have been horrified to see that... *(To* MAY*)* And you, May... *(To* SALLY*)* And beer.

(Lights fade.)

5.
Running Away.

(The same. A short time later)

(IRENIE, SALLY, MAY, DAVID *and* LUCY:)

IRENIE: Kate, she seems really good for Rose... They've known each other for like six months?

SALLY: As a couple.

LUCY: They came into the city to see me. Last April. Was I surprised...

IRENIE: She hadn't told you.

LUCY: My high school history teacher...

SALLY: *(To* IRENIE*)* Think what that's been like for Kate.

IRENIE: What do you mean?

SALLY: Rose said when she told her... They'd been together two months.

DAVID: A little less I think when she was told.

SALLY: And Kate then ran away for a while.

IRENIE: Where?

SALLY: To some retreat where you hardly speak. You're silent. Rose thought there was a very good chance that she'd never hear from Kate again. She's still here.

DAVID: Good for her.

LUCY: What is Mom doing?

SALLY: She went for a walk. She'll be back.

LUCY: Dad, last night I came downstairs... I'd heard a voice. Mom was here in the kitchen. Sitting right here. Talking. At first I don't think she knew who I was.

DAVID: She's half asleep...

SALLY: Was she on her computer?

LUCY: No. Not this time. I told her I'd decided to not accept the residency.

DAVID: Lucy, don't—.

LUCY: I thought maybe she'd like that. But she just covers her ears and says, 'I'm not going to talk about it. I'm not going to talk about it. You're going. You're going.'

DAVID: Life can't stop...

IRENIE: This is the residency in France?

LUCY: I don't want to be away...

IRENIE: I can understand that.

DAVID: I understand too. But it doesn't start until January. And there's no reason to feel guilty.

SALLY: It's a big thing. There's a festival at the end of it.

MAY: There was a notice up about it at Gibney, I think. How to apply...

IRENIE: I saw that too.

DAVID: All paid for. Jacques Francois says he'll look after you. He happens to teach part time there at the school.

MAY: Who's—?

SALLY: The very first man we ever let into Rose's company, May.

IRENIE: So we finally got to do lifts...

SALLY: He snuck in with his sister. Great feet.

DAVID: *(To* LUCY*)* Who knows what's going to happen with your Mom. Or when? We can't just stop our lives.

IRENIE: *(To* LUCY*)* Eight months in France. I'm jealous. *I should run away.*

LUCY: It's not running away, Irenie—.

IRENIE: I didn't mean…

DAVID: She's not running away.

SALLY: *(Over this)* Irenie…

IRENIE: That's not what I meant. I meant me. I was talking about me. *(Then)* You ever been to Europe, May?

MAY: Once, right after school. A group of us went over to audition. One guy got a job in Stuttgart. That was it. I got into debt. But it was fun. Lucy will have a good time. I'm jealous.

DAVID: Hear that, Lucy?

SALLY: David, let's move that table. We're too many… Rose usually does that.

DAVID: She hasn't for a while.

(SALLY *and* DAVID *move the table.*)

LUCY: Dad, we've been going through Mom's things for the exhibit. It's all in the living room. If we're just sitting here… *(To* MAY*)* Let's go. *(She gets up.)*

DAVID: Bring them here. Bring them. Stay in here.

LUCY: Dad—

DAVID: Do it in here.

LUCY: There are like ten boxes, Dad.

DAVID: Bring a box. Two. Show Irenie what you've been discovering… It's neat what they've been finding. Come back in here…

LUCY: Okay, Dad.

(LUCY *and* MAY *go off.*)

DAVID: Maybe she shouldn't go.

SALLY: It's what Rose wants. She's been very clear.

DAVID: *(Over this)* Maybe she shouldn't be away. Maybe she needs to be home.

IRENIE: And what does Lucy want?

DAVID: And maybe it's not even the right time.

IRENIE: What do you mean?

DAVID: Europe now. I was in Paris last spring and I saw this play. The main character's this crazy Trump-like figure—really gross, you know, all of that. Fat. Funny colored hair. A total clown. With tantrums and hamburgers… He's always throwing things. Breaking things. Sticking his hand down his pants. Grabbing at girls'… There was another character dressed perfectly as Kermit the Frog.

IRENIE: Why Kermit the Frog?

DAVID: I have no idea.

IRENIE: I love Kermit.

DAVID: And this Kermit wears an army helmet. Walks around with a machine gun… Another guy dressed as a Klansman—. He holds a big cross and wears a suicide vest. All the time the actors are screaming at the audience, pretending, I suppose, to be loud Americans. Won every theater award. They want me to help bring it to New York…

IRENIE: I see that too, David. There was a dancer visiting at Gibney; he was German. He kept commiserating with the other dancers, the American dancers, 'I know, oh I know what it's like for you Americans now. With him…'

DAVID: Trump.

IRENIE: *(Over this)* 'I had to spend so much of my youth apologizing for my Nazi parents.'

DAVID: And killing al-Baghdadi won't change any minds. It's so different than when we toured Europe.

IRENIE: I do want to run away, Sally. Every day I feel that more and more… Or is that just getting old?

(KATE *returns with things for the quiche.*)

KATE: She's sitting outside. I dried off the bench. She'll come in when she's ready.

(Timer goes off.)

IRENIE: Sure…

(KATE *will take the crust out of the oven.*)

DAVID: It smells so good.

KATE: It's just the crust. *(Then)* She told me she has an appointment to have the growth removed. She wants you all to know that.

SALLY: When?

KATE: I don't know.

DAVID: That's good. If she needs a ride… If I'm not here, Sally…

SALLY: Kate drives… What else can we do…? We're just sitting here, Kate.

KATE: The…?

SALLY: We want to do something. Please.

KATE: Okay. Salads…?

SALLY: The salads. From recipes…?

KATE: *(Handing her the recipes)* Right here…

SALLY: Of course they're from recipes… She's Kate.

KATE: In the bags… Lettuce is in the refrigerator, already washed… I bought that at Tops.

SALLY: David, this one, you do this one...

IRENIE: And me?

DAVID: You're the guest...

(KATE *will work on the quiche filling.*)

SALLY: I'd love to run away from here, Irenie... Rhinebeck.

IRENIE: What do you mean? Why would you do that?

SALLY: David and I talk about that all the time.

DAVID: It's just talk.

KATE: And go where?

SALLY: Way out into the country, Kate.

IRENIE: I thought this was the country. *This* is where people run to.

DAVID: Not any more, Irenie. Not people who aren't rich.

SALLY: You know. I take the garbage out to the road. And who's walking down our quiet little one-lane country road? Van Jones. *The* Van Jones.

KATE: Who's Van...?

IRENIE: The CNN Van Jones. You don't watch CNN? What do you watch, Kate, MSNBC?

SALLY: He's been on Maddow I think.

DAVID: Probably visiting Omega, Sally.

SALLY: When David and I can't even afford to eat out in our own village...

(ROSE *appears.*)

DAVID: Rose...

KATE: You all right?

ROSE: I am.

DAVID: Join us.

KATE: You want to help cook?

ROSE: No.

SALLY: We are just talking about running away, Rose. Getting the hell out and starting all over again.

ROSE: Let me grab my running shoes… I'm all in.

SALLY: Remember when we all ran away? That summer? Ran away with you, Rose.

IRENIE: To that fucking barn. Way out in—. Where was it? I'll never get over it.

ROSE: Near Utica.

SALLY: *(To* ROSE*)* You and Alice… Just the four of us. All summer.

(LUCY *and* MAY *have returned with some large accordian files and a box.)*

LUCY: You're back, Mom.

IRENIE: And you, Lucy.

LUCY: Me what?

SALLY: Your Mom had just had you, Lucy…

IRENIE: A big barn, crappy beds. Everything smelled.

SALLY: Nature.

LUCY: What are you talking about?

DAVID: One summer. When they ran away.

IRENIE: Straw beds. Made of real straw.

DAVID: I wasn't there. I wasn't welcome then.

(DAVID *goes off to the pantry.)*

ROSE: *(To* DAVID*)* We weren't back to talking to each other. We had just…

SALLY: A wood floor. No mirrors. She hates mirrors.

ROSE: I do.

LUCY: I know. When was this?

SALLY: Lucy, you were maybe one year old. Way the hell out in the country.

IRENIE: And no bathrooms. Think of it.

SALLY: May, the only rule we dancers had was—

IRENIE & SALLY: —'don't step on the baby'.

ROSE: *(To* LUCY*)* Don't step on you.

IRENIE: *(To* LUCY*)* That was it. The rule.

LUCY: I've never heard this…

(DAVID *will return with the lettuce and salad bowls.)*

ROSE: Alice kept complaining: 'It's the summer of all that's happening in the world, in China and elsewhere, and we're… here. Nowhere. Near Utica. What are we doing dancing?' *(Then)* I'd go back there in a second. I'd run away back there right now…

(LUCY *and* MAY *will begin to go through the files.* DAVID *and* SALLY *work on the salad,* KATE *on the quiche.)*

IRENIE: Where would you run away to, Kate?

ROSE: Kate's not going anywhere. She's going to stay right here with me. Aren't you? I'm not letting go of her…

(KATE *smiles.)*

ROSE: She's way too dug in here, aren't you?

KATE: I suppose I am.

IRENIE: In where?

ROSE: Rhinebeck… Show them the photos you showed me this morning at the market.

KATE: Why do you want me to—?

ROSE: *(Over this)* Do you have them? Where are they? In your purse? Where's your purse?

KATE: Yeah.

(KATE *points out her purse.* ROSE *goes to* KATE'*s purse.)*

DAVID: Photos of what?

ROSE: I want them to see. You'll see… She has a real life.

KATE: What does that mean?

(ROSE *takes out a pile of photos.)*

SALLY: She get prints made. We're going to lose all of our photos…

ROSE: Look at these. Look. Here…

(ROSE *hands a photo to* DAVID.*)*

ROSE: David, look at *him*… *(Shows a photo)*

DAVID: And who's that?

ROSE: Tell them.

KATE: A student of mine.

IRENIE: I thought you retired.

ROSE: She teaches E S L. She volunteers. *(Pointing)* That's the moment her student became a citizen. Right?

KATE: *(Nods)* I'd never been to one of these before. And I'd never seen this man in a suit. It didn't fit him…

SALLY: May I see?

KATE: I think his wife gave him the haircut. After, everyone took photos with the judge.

ROSE: Here… Lucy?

(Another photo)

KATE: I've bored the girls already. They've seen them.

LUCY: Only a few of them. Let me see.

(LUCY *is handed a pile of photos.*)

ROSE: *(Explains the photo)* Kate says there's a car dealership in Poughkeepsie that donates those little flags.

SALLY: Can I see that one? *(To* IRENIE*)* Here…

(Photos begin to be passed around.)

KATE: *(Pointing out)* His daughter. His wife.

ROSE: Look at the faces…

LUCY: They're really great.

KATE: *(Points to a photo)* That man is his friend… From the same Mexican town. *(To* ROSE*)* He's the one who had the accident in the spring. *(To the others)* There was insurance to sort out for him. I don't know so much about insurance…

MAY: *(To* LUCY, *with a photo)* Look at her. She's probably my age.

DAVID: *(Looking at a photo)* I cancelled one of my tours this year. A Dutch theater company –had consulate money and everything—one of their actors can't get a visa.

IRENIE: From Holland??

DAVID: Originally from Afghanistan—.

ROSE: *(With a photo, to* KATE*)* When was this?

KATE: The ceremony? Monday.

ROSE: I hadn't seen these until this morning…

KATE: I haven't been around that much all week, remember? I stayed away to give you time with your daughter and niece. I have absolutely no training…

ROSE: You were a teacher.

KATE: You talk to them. Make up exercises. Play word games. Hope you're helpful. Some of it is just life stuff—rental contracts, school things.

DAVID: *(With the photos)* Where was this held? The ceremony?

(KATE smiles.)

ROSE: What?

KATE: In the village hall basement, in—Hopewell Junction. Nice name, right?

DAVID: Very nice. *(Showing the others)* His son waving the flag...

KATE: They've got four kids....

ROSE: Kate says they ride bikes.

SALLY: I've seen them on bikes in the village.

LUCY: Me too.

KATE: They don't dare drive.

ROSE: Kate is Ms. Rhinebeck!

KATE: I am not, Rose—

ROSE: *(Over this)* Everywhere we go. Stickles, the CVS. Everyone: hi, Kate. Hi! Hi!

LUCY: It's true.

KATE: I taught them. Everyone.

ROSE: We get lost in our own little world, Irenie.

SALLY: What else does she volunteer for?

ROSE: I can hardly keep track...

KATE: Not as many as others I know...

DAVID: *(To SALLY)* She's finding things to do. She just retired.

KATE: I've been teaching these adults for years, David.

SALLY: She didn't just start because she retired.

ROSE: *(Beginning a list)* Kate teaches immigrants English; she volunteers at the library—.

KATE: Just for the book sales.

ROSE: Tell them what you do at the historical society. She's like the secretary…

KATE: I am the secretary.

SALLY: You put us all to shame.

KATE: *(To SALLY, over this)* You teach—.

SALLY: Little kids to dance. Mostly it's for the moms. And I'm probably going to have to give up my studio—it's gotten so goddamn expensive. Rhinebeck.

(KATE *has poured the quiche filling into the crust, and begins to pick it up.*)

ROSE: Could someone help, Kate—?

DAVID: I got it. Look at that… *(The quiche)*

SALLY: Looks wonderful.

ROSE: Don't spill. Don't spill. That's our dinner. She's a genius.

KATE: Only to someone who never cooks, Rose. *(She has put the quiche in the oven.)* Now we wait. There's cheese and bread.

ROSE: Kate, that song you sang when we were walking along the lake last week. Will you sing it?

KATE: Okay… *(Sings)*
Vayse, broyne, shvartse, gele—
Misht di farbn oys tsuzamen
Ale mentshn zaynen brider,
It's Yiddish. *(Sings a translation:)*
White, brown, black, yellow
Mix the colors all together

All men are brothers
From one father from one mother

ROSE: *(Explains)* She went here!

SALLY: Where??

DAVID: *(Over this)* What are you talking about?

ROSE: *(Over this)* I couldn't believe it when she told me.

DAVID: What??

ROSE: Right here, David. Where we're sitting.

KATE: The summer camp that was here. On this property and all around the lake. All this used to be a summer camp...

SALLY: We know.

LUCY: *(Same time)* I knew that.

KATE: And I went here. As a kid, Lucy.

LUCY: You're kidding.

DAVID: You went here?

KATE: Camp Boiberik, it was called. It'd been here for years and years. Something like sixty years.

ROSE: They still have reunions...

KATE: [the song in her head] It's a very corny song... 'We're all brothers.' From another time... A *secular* Yiddish summer camp for kids. That's they said it was.

DAVID: What the hell is that?

SALLY: So it wasn't religious.

KATE: 'Creating rituals not religion.' That was one of its slogans. It had a lot of slogans.

It was a summer camp.

IRENIE: She went here?

SALLY: She just told us that.

KATE: My parents would put my brother and me on a boat—up the Hudson, to Poughkeepsie. *(Amazed)* We came by boat from New York City.

LUCY: Huh.

KATE: *(Over this)* Every day, weather permitting, we swam in your lake…

ROSE: And the girls all wore white dresses.

LUCY: Why?

KATE: *(Over this)* On Fridays, Rose, when we'd sing that together.

ROSE: The Omega—our good neighbors—they bought the camp…

KATE: Bought everything except your two houses. Why we don't know. How that happened.

ROSE: And tell them what you told me, Kate. About Omega. Where all that comes from. You know-

KATE: Rose liked this. I was working on a display, for the Post Office, about Omega celebrating its thirtieth year, I think; and I dug through a lot of stuff from the Historical Society. And I remembered something I learned doing this. So I told Rose; I thought she'd be interested and she really was. I learned that Omega—the institute—comes out of the religion of Sufism.

DAVID: I didn't know that. I had no idea.

SALLY: I'd heard that.

KATE: So doing the display I researched a little bit about Sufism, which, I learned—was born out of very very difficult times.

SALLY: It was. I know this.

KATE: *(Over this)* A time of plagues, and famines, corruptions, and all sorts of terrible things. And into this miserable world came this new religion, which, had for its heart, at its center, its core—. And this is what Rose loved: *(Then)* Dance.

ROSE: Dance!

DAVID: You're kidding.

LUCY: *(Same time)* Is that true?

SALLY: It's true.

MAY: *(Same time)* Dance?

SALLY: *(Over this)* And dance, not just as something to be appreciated and watched.

KATE: *(To* SALLY*)* You knew this.

SALLY: *(Over this)* I studied this. For Sufis, it's how they worship.

IRENIE: I think I've heard this.

ROSE: Dance. Singing. Coming out of bad times…

KATE: I told some of my fellow singers in chorus; they were amazed.

SALLY: In what?

ROSE: She's in a chorus.

KATE: At Bard. The community chorus. I should get the crepes.

SALLY: *(To* DAVID*)* Why don't I know this? We've lived here for twenty years. I like to sing.

KATE: *(To* SALLY*)* All kinds of people are in it. Other teachers. Barbara Apple—she taught you too, Lucy, I think.

LUCY: Eleventh grade English.

KATE: We sometimes carpool. *(She goes off to the pantry.)*

SALLY: *(To* DAVID*)* Why don't I know about this?

IRENIE: *(To* ROSE*)* You're showing her off.

ROSE: She doesn't know our world…I'd worried she'd feel a little awkward… She's such an interesting woman.

IRENIE: Even though she's not a dancer.

ROSE: Even though she's not a dancer.

(KATE *returns with the crepes:*)

KATE: I took Rose with me to my book club…

SALLY: *(To* DAVID*)* She belongs to a book club.

KATE: *(To* ROSE*)* May I tell them about this? I think they'd like to hear this…

DAVID: What?

KATE: The book club meets at the Rhinecliff library. Sometimes we watch a movie instead of talking about a book. Last week, when I took Rose, we happened to watch a movie. About a man who'd worked in a government office for years and years; his life that of a cold bureaucrat. Some mothers come in and want to create a park for their kids. He doesn't even listen, moves them on. Then he learns that he's got cancer, and he's dying. I hadn't known what the movie was going to be about… *(To* ROSE*)* That's true… *(Then)* Of course he completely changes. First he gets drunk, panics, feels sorry for himself—. When he suddenly remembers the park. And begins to fight for it. Fight the bureaucracy that he had been such a part of. A kids' little park with swings. And it gets built, and then, he dies. *(Then)* We all discussed it after. We always do. Rose participated.

ROSE: I did.

KATE: What did you tell everyone?

ROSE: I told them I was dying.

KATE: I don't think you'd said that to anyone 'publicly' before. Had you? I'm not sure you'd ever actually said it to me. First time. You didn't even know some of these women…

ROSE: No.

KATE: Maybe that made it easier?

ROSE: Maybe…

KATE: *(To* ROSE*)* It felt like a big step…

ROSE: It did, Kate.

(Lights fade.)

6.
Mother and Daughter.

(The same. A short time later. LUCY *and* MAY *hold up an IPhone to* IRENIE. SALLY *and* DAVID *are finishing making the salads.)*

(On the IPhone a video plays of a rehearsal of one of ROSE's *dances:* LUCY *is dancing this in the video.)*

*(*KATE *will spread Nutella on the crepes and carefully fold them.* ROSE *sits with* KATE.*)*

(Faint music [Scott Joplin's Maple Leaf Rag*] plays on the IPhone:)*

ROSE: Irenie, someone gave me a mug the other day.

KATE: My friend, Marian. She doesn't know about you, Rose.

ROSE: With this written on it: "I'm not aging, I'm ripening."

LUCY: *(The video)* Here, Irenie. Right here. Just watch this…

DAVID: I like that. I want a mug like that.

ROSE: You can have mine.

SALLY: *(As she works, about the video)* Is that right? The turn...

(They watch.)

SALLY: Her sort of look—that's to the audience? Is that what you did? Play it again.

(LUCY plays it again.)

LUCY: That's what I'm doing. Let's show her again...

(ROSE Looks toward the girls, then:)

ROSE: May I see too? *(The video)*

(The others stop.)

ROSE: May I see?

LUCY: Of course, Mom. Sure. I'd love you to take a look. You'll look at it?

IRENIE: Take it to her...

ROSE: I'm coming. *(She comes to the others to watch the video.)*

IRENIE: It's been so long since I've seen this dance, Rose. You put a little of everything in it. Merce, Taylor... *(To* MAY*)* She's making fun of ballet...

MAY: With the hands. I know.

ROSE: *(To* LUCY*)* What am I looking at?

LUCY: It's from this morning.

SALLY: They film each other every day, Rose. If only we could have done that.

LUCY: What I've been anxious to ask Irenie is... And you, Mom... Wait a minute. Here... I was just showing her. Let me stop it...

ROSE: Don't stop.

LUCY: Mom, we're past the...

ROSE: Leave it, I'm watching.

(As ROSE *watches:*)

IRENIE: Rose, I'm trying to remember why I did what I did. What the hell was I doing?

SALLY: We'll look tomorrow at the old videos.

MAY: You're really dark in them, Irenie…

LUCY: She, on the tape, does something, Mom. In Irenie's tape you hear the audience laugh. But I can't see what she what was doing…

SALLY: Tomorrow we'll look at the old video. They're in the studio…

LUCY: *(Watching the video with* ROSE*)* I was late on the one there… I know that. I know.

ROSE: Who does the filming—?

LUCY: May.

MAY: And Lucy videos me in my solo. And for the duet… *(Smiles)*

ROSE: What, May?

MAY: We scotch tape the phone onto a box. A couple of times it slipped—

LUCY: We filmed the ceiling.

ROSE: How do you stop this thing?

LUCY: Here…I'll do it. This…I'll do it.

(LUCY *stops the music.* ROSE *looks over the IPhone and sets it down.*)

IRENIE: We needed one of those…

LUCY: So, Mom—

ROSE: What?

LUCY: Now that you have finally seen a little of what we've been doing… Tomorrow we're hoping to show you—and Irenie—all three dances. Okay? In Sally's studio… You going to do that? Will you do that?

(No response)

IRENIE: *(A joke)* You even remember that dance, Rose?

ROSE: *(To* LUCY*)* Can you show me where you're having the problem?

LUCY: *(Surprised)* Now? Sure. And any advice…

ROSE: Show me the whole thing…

LUCY: *(To the others as a joke)* From the horse's mouth. Can't do better than that… *(She starts to find it on the phone.)*

ROSE: Not on that thing, Lucy.

LUCY: What, Mom?

ROSE: Can you show me?

LUCY: Show you what?

ROSE: I think I'll need to see the whole thing. Can you do that? Here.

LUCY: In here? It's the kitchen…

ROSE: Then never mind.

LUCY: No, no, I'm happy to, Mom… Of course. Sure. *(To* MAY*)* In the kitchen.

ROSE: Maybe you just want Irenie to help you…

LUCY: Of course not. Mom, of course not. Obviously. It's your dance. They're all your dances… It's what I've been asking.

(No one has anything to say, this is a real mother-daughter time.)

ROSE: So…

LUCY: Okay.

ROSE: Take off your shoes.

LUCY: I was going to.

ROSE: You dance in your bare feet.

LUCY: I know. I know that. *(She sits, takes off her shoes, socks.)* May, please move things… *(Chairs, etc)*

MAY: *(To* DAVID *who stands to help)* I've got it, David…

DAVID: Where should I…?

SALLY: Out of the way?

DAVID: Where's that?

IRENIE: Lucy, where…?

LUCY: Close to the table.

*(*MAY *moves a chair or two out of the way.)*

ROSE: So where is this big problem? Where are you lost?

LUCY: I don't feel lost. I didn't say that.

ROSE: Show me. Come on.

LUCY: *(Taking off her shoes)* I will. I am about to. Mom let me get—. Dad, will you… *(Telling him where to sit)* Is this enough room?

ROSE: Don't worry about the facings. Just fit it in.

MAY: We've changed the facings, Aunt Rose. We're in the round.

ROSE: In the round?

SALLY: I told you that. That's how they've set it up at the Lumberyard.

ROSE: *(To* SALLY*)* Is she doing it dancy?

LUCY: I'm not doing it 'dancy', Mom.

ROSE: *(To* SALLY*)* All that ballet. *(To* DAVID*)* I didn't want her to study that.

DAVID: She wanted to, Rose.

ROSE: *(To* LUCY*)* You sure there's enough room?

LUCY: There isn't.

ROSE: *(Ignores her)* Where do you want me?

LUCY: Wherever. Okay. Couldn't I just show you the spots where—?

ROSE: From the beginning.

LUCY: From the beginning? May? Can you…?

(LUCY *hands* MAY *the phone. She takes a deep breath.*)

LUCY: There's not enough room.

ROSE: Are your shoes in the way?

DAVID: I got them… *(He grabs* LUCY*'s shoes…)*

ROSE: Ready?

(LUCY *nods to* MAY)

MAY: And…

(MAY *puts on the music: Scott Joplin's Maple Leaf Rag.*)

(LUCY *starts dancing.*)

ROSE: Listen. Are you listening…?

LUCY: *(As she dances, tries to speak)* I'm listening, Mom.

ROSE: *(Claps her hands)* Stop. Stop.

(LUCY *stops dancing:*)

LUCY: I'm listening to you.

ROSE: Not to me. To the music. *(To* SALLY*)* Is she still operating on counts or on the music?

SALLY: I don't know.

ROSE: Listen to the music, Lucy.

IRENIE: *(Gestures for* MAY *to stop the music)* May…

(MAY *stops the music.*)

ROSE: *(To* LUCY*)* What's the name of this dance? Do you know?

LUCY: Of course I know, Mom. I'm just trying to do your steps and—.

ROSE: Kate?

KATE: *(Surprised)* What??

ROSE: This dance, what I named it: *My Brokenhearted Rag.* That's not the title of the music, it's the title I gave to this dance.

(Everyone is silent.)

ROSE: So anyone who dances it—and this can be danced by man or woman—is heartbroken.

LUCY: I'll try, Mom. I'll try to do that. *(Smiles to* MAY*)*

ROSE: It's not funny.

LUCY: I'm sorry. Can we try it again?

ROSE: Don't make faces at May… *(She thinks, then:)* I made that when Alice had left us. Remember when she left us?

LUCY: Sure.

ROSE: You didn't know that.

LUCY: No.

ROSE: You knew, Irenie. You danced it.

IRENIE: I remember now you telling me that. I'd forgotten.

ROSE: Kate, Alice had met a young costume designer. Alice always liked clothes. But she was still doing my lights, so I asked her to come to rehearsal and see what we were doing. We weren't talking. And then she came and sat in the back of the church where we were working. And Irenie, you danced this. Beautifully.

IRENIE: Thank you.

ROSE: And after you'd finished, I hear this voice shouting from the back, "so what do you call it, Rose?" No compliment. No nothing. Just "what do you call it, Rose?" So I shout back, and it just comes, just came out, I made it up on the spot: "Alice, I call it *My Broken Hearted Rag*."

DAVID: I didn't know that.

ROSE: You still weren't talking to me then, David.

LUCY: But she came back, Mom. Alice.

ROSE: Not forever.

LUCY: Only because she died.

(ROSE *looks at* LUCY:)

ROSE: Do it again. Let's see the whole damn thing. This time don't stop. Don't give up.

LUCY: You stopped me.

DAVID: They're going to show you everything in Sally's studio tomorrow. It's a dance studio.

ROSE: *(To* LUCY*)* You've learned the whole thing?

LUCY: *(Over the end of this)* Of course I have. We've been rehearsing for weeks.

ROSE: Can you do it? If you can do it, do it. May, can you do that music thing again...?

LUCY: I'm going to move this. *(A rug)* I was tripping... Help me, Dad.

(DAVID *helps* LUCY.)

ROSE: *(To the others)* I was just thinking about Alice. There's a lot of stuff of hers in those... [the files]

MAY: Yeh. There is.

ROSE: *(To* LUCY*)* You seem worried.

LUCY: It's fine. I'm not 'worried.'

ROSE: *(Smiles)* Good. Good... That's more like it. May...? And not too dancy. And listen... Listen.

LUCY: I'm going to do the entrance.

ROSE: Lucy, heartbroken... And when your heart breaks, you keep moving and dance. Fast.

MAY: Ready? And...

(MAY *puts on the music/video.*)

(LUCY *dances.* ROSE *watches and soon gets lost in her own memories.*)

ROSE: *(To* SALLY*)* Was she late on the one?

SALLY: No.

(LUCY *dances. She nearly runs into* ROSE:)

LUCY: Get out of my way, Mom. Sorry, you were in my way...

(LUCY *has to move* ROSE *out of the way, she stops her dance for a moment, and then picks it up again.*)

LUCY: *(Dancing)* It's really fast, Mom. *(She dances.)*

ROSE: *(To* IRENIE*)* The Paul Taylor thing.

IRENIE: I know.

(LUCY *dances.*)

LUCY: *(As she dances, about a moment of the dance)* Broken hearted...

(LUCY *dances.*)

ROSE: I keep seeing you, Irenie.

(LUCY *dances.*)

ROSE: The little guy there is very Graham.

IRENIE: It is.

(LUCY *finishes the dance. She is out of breath. Without a pause:*)

ROSE: The facings are all different—.

LUCY: We're in a kitchen.

SALLY: And they'll be doing it in the round.

ROSE: You have to keep off the classical line.

SALLY: I think she's doing that.

ROSE: David, those goddamn ballet classes.

LUCY: *(Out of breath)* Tell me where I'm not…

ROSE: And at the end: the slap-slap? Then relax. The other is Graham. *(She turns back to the others:)* That's a nice little dance… *(To* LUCY*)* You can dance that when you go to France.

DAVID: Lucy, that was great. Really great.

ROSE: What's next? May?

(All look at MAY, *now on the spot, who starts to take off her shoes and socks.)*

ROSE: *(To* LUCY*)* What did we choose for her?

LUCY: *(Still out of breath) Blue Eyed Blues,* Mom.

ROSE: *(To* MAY*)* Oh that's not easy, is it?

MAY: *(Taking off her shoes)* No.

LUCY: *(Out of breath)* She's doing good. I think.

ROSE: *(To* SALLY*)* You didn't dance that.

SALLY: No.

ROSE: Who's been teaching—?

LUCY: I have. Off the video. You want to see what she's been—? *(She picks up the phone.)*

ROSE: You just play the music. Can you do that? And May's going to show me. Aren't you, May?

MAY: I hope so.

ROSE: Please, be more confident than that.

MAY: I'll show you.

ROSE: *(To* SALLY*)* Who's on the old video?

SALLY: Julie danced this.

ROSE: Who'd she learn it from?

SALLY: I don't remember.

IRENIE: *(A joke)* Rose, whose blue eyes? Someone we knew?

DAVID: *(A joke)* Not me.

ROSE: No, David, not you.

IRENIE: I've always wanted to ask. Alice didn't have blue eyes.

ROSE: No. No, she didn't. *(To* MAY*)* Enough room? Not too crowded?

MAY: It's fine.

ROSE: Good. Lucy, see May doesn't complain.

MAY: I can even rehearse this in my bedroom…

ROSE: Good. Hear that, Lucy?

(As they wait, MAY *puts up her hair into a bun:)*

MAY: Sorry, I washed my hair last night, I need to double tie my bun.

ROSE: We'll wait… We'll wait.

*(*MAY *ties her bun.)*

ROSE: Bun all tied up? Good. I made this dance on me, Kate.

KATE: What does that mean?

DAVID: She made it on herself to dance.

KATE: You danced this?

ROSE: I did, Kate. I did. *(To* LUCY*)* And you've been teaching her?

LUCY: Yes, Mom.

ROSE: This will be interesting.

SALLY: They haven't finished...

ROSE: Don't apologize...

SALLY: I wasn't...

ROSE: Sh-sh.

(MAY *looks to* LUCY *and nods.*)

LUCY: And...

(LUCY *puts on the IPhone music, again it is quiet:* Crazy Blue Eyes *by Lacy J Dalton.*)

(MAY *dances;* LUCY, *while sitting, will do some of the gestures of the dance along with* MAY.)

ROSE: Lucy, there's a move on every count.

LUCY: I know. I know.

(MAY *dances.*)

ROSE: *(Again, to* SALLY*)* Who did Julie learn it from?

SALLY: I told you, I don't know.

(MAY *dances.*)

IRENIE: Now I'm seeing you...

(MAY *dances.*)

ROSE: I haven't seen this dance for, it must be, thirty years.

(MAY *dances.*)

ROSE: *(To* MAY*)* Go for it. It still hurts. *(To* KATE*)* She's had it with those jerky blue eyes...

(MAY *finishes.*)

ROSE: She's even more pissed off at those blue eyes. She's really angry, Lucy.

LUCY: Okay. Okay.

MAY: *(Out of breath)* I thought I was late, so I tried to make up for it...

ROSE: *(To* LUCY*)* Was she late?

LUCY: I don't think you were.

MAY: *(Over this, showing)* If you don't get on the left foot it's over. The slide—I don't do well in Taylor with this either...

(Lights fade.)

7.
Rose Michael & Company.

(The same. A short time later)

*(*DAVID, ROSE, *and* IRENIE *dig through the old files.* KATE *folds the crepes.* SALLY *takes a loaf of French bread and she will slice it so it can be buttered.)*

DAVID: *(With a photo)* Rose, who's this?

LUCY: Give us ten minutes, Sally.

*(*LUCY *and* MAY *go off to the living room.)*

SALLY: Tell us if you want us in the living room...

ROSE: *(About the photo)* I don't know. Irenie...?

IRENIE: Let me see.

DAVID: *(Another photo)* Oh Rose...

SALLY: *(To* DAVID*)* What one's that? What are you showing her?

ROSE: *(About the photo)* Kate, this was when it had gotten really hard for Sally to keep her clothes on.

SALLY: Why are you telling her that?

IRENIE: Let me see.

SALLY: Dig a little deeper in that box and find some 'nice' photos of Rose.

ROSE: I think we've filed all those away already... *(Half to herself)* Circular file...

IRENIE: You got any of me?

DAVID: *(Shows ROSE and KATE)* Here's another one...

ROSE: *(With the photo)* See, she'd take her clothes off at the drop of a hat...

KATE: Is that true?

SALLY: What are you showing them?

IRENIE: Let us see.

(SALLY, *to* DAVID *who is smiling:*)

SALLY: Come on. And I wasn't as bad as Dwayne.

ROSE: This is true.

KATE: Dwayne?

SALLY: *(To DAVID)* Remember...?

IRENIE: *(To KATE)* Dwayne was a dancer... Is. Maybe still is. I don't know.

SALLY: He wasn't in the company. We just used him when we had to.

ROSE: We did.

DAVID: *(To SALLY)* What were you saying about Dwayne?

SALLY: At Judson, I think.

IRENIE: *(To KATE)* Where we danced.

SALLY: *(Over this)* We haven't been dancing for more than say five minutes, Kate, and Dwayne starts to unbutton his shirt. He's like, only on his second button, when someone—

DAVID: I was there. I remember this.

SALLY: —in the first row I think, someone says, and very, very loudly— 'not again!'

KATE: May I see?

SALLY: I was thinner then...

(KATE *is handed the photo of* SALLY.)

ROSE: *(Another)* Kate, here's me—I'm still dancing. Have I shown you any of these?

KATE: No. No. *That's* you...?

ROSE: You questioning that?

KATE: *(Smiles)* No!

ROSE: *(Not completely joking)* You better not be.

DAVID: The rest of this is Alice's stuff...

KATE: May I see some of Alice's 'stuff?' *(She will look at the pile of Alice's photos, etc.)*

IRENIE: *(Looking at Alice's stuff too)* You know they should do a display for Alice too...

SALLY: What do you think, Rose?

IRENIE: She was such an important part of our world.

SALLY: She was...

ROSE: She was a star...

DAVID: *(With a photo)* Merce...?

(They turn their attention to the photo; KATE *gets lost in Alice's stuff.)*

IRENIE: Merce...

ROSE: *(Taking the photo from* DAVID*)* That's him. Let me see. *(Looking at the photo of Merce Cunningham)* Kate, I once asked him "How come you create so many dances as quartets and quintets? Is it some kind of numbers thing?" I knew he liked playing with numbers. But he said— 'no, it's not that, it's because that's how many people fit into my station wagon…'

DAVID: They were always touring.

ROSE: Look at this, Sally…

DAVID: In his station wagon… *(To* ROSE*)* I got a ride in that once… *(Shakes his head. Other photos)* Rose…

ROSE: *(The photos)* I didn't know we had these. You have kept them.

DAVID: I did. I gave them to Lucy for your display… She knew nothing about them.

IRENIE: What are they?

*(*DAVID *shows* IRENIE.*)*

IRENIE: What is that?

DAVID: You don't know.

ROSE: That was way before these two, David. We were kids. Just you and me.

DAVID: We certainly were kids.

KATE: *(Putting down Alice's stuff)* Let me put some of this back in the fridge.

*(*KATE *heads off to the pantry;* ROSE *watches her go.)*

DAVID: I don't know if either of you are aware of this—but Rose Michael can on occasion get just a little obsessed with things.

IRENIE: Oh really?

SALLY: 'I'm shocked.'

ROSE: Shut up. Why is Kate in there by herself? She should be out here.

SALLY: She's getting things. Doing stuff. It's her dinner… She's busy…

DAVID: *(The photo)* This was one those 'obsessions'. A dance—and I use that word in the broadest definition—based upon some movie Rose had fallen in love with—where, at the Thalia?

ROSE: Probably.

DAVID: A five-and-a-half hour movie. About a woman doing mostly very normal things. She makes a meal, step by step, in real time, very slowly.

IRENIE: I think I know this movie.

DAVID: *(Over this)* Sets a table, eats.

ROSE: Washes dishes.

DAVID: Goes into her bedroom, lays a towel on the bed, answers the door, a man is there, he follows her—

ROSE: Unbuckling his belt,

DAVID: —into her bedroom, she closes the door. Door opens, they come out, he hands her money, he goes, she puts the money on the dining room table.

ROSE: In a vase on the table.

DAVID: And that's pretty much the movie. And that is what Rose made into a—dance.

(ROSE *gets up.*)

SALLY: Where are you going?

(ROSE *goes.*)

IRENIE: How long was her dance?

DAVID: Five and a half hours. Obsessed. And with no intermission. No bathroom break. She did have a little bucket just off stage. And a microphone so the audience, could hear...

IRENIE: You're making that up.

DAVID: She said, she wanted to make sure there was always something happening.

SALLY: I love her.

DAVID: *(Over this)* When it finally ended—thank you god—there were just three left in the audience. And Rose *(Smiles)* instead of taking a bow, she goes right up to each of the courageous or insane or homeless three and shakes their hand and says—'thanks for coming, let's stay in touch!'

(Laughter)

SALLY: *(To* IRENIE*)* You've never heard this either.

IRENIE: No.

DAVID: *(Over this)* They all still send Christmas cards...

IRENIE: Is that a joke?

(ROSE *leads* KATE *out of the pantry:*)

ROSE: They will be interested... Show them... She did it for me in the pantry. She still remembers. She danced right here...

KATE: As a kid.

OTHERS: What?? What are you talking about?

ROSE: *(Over this)* They wore tiny bells on ankle bracelets.

KATE: When this was a kids' camp. They had something called 'felker yontif'. All the kids were assigned a nation. I was Russia...

OTHERS: Do it! Show us! Russia! Come on, Kate.

ROSE: *(Over this)* Let's show them.

KATE: I'm not a dancer... You're dancers... We danced here.

(KATE *does a few steps then stops;* LUCY *and* MAY *return during the 'dance'.*)

DAVID: Kate danced here, Lucy.

LUCY: Really?

IRENIE: Years and years ago.

LUCY: Great. I think we're ready.

MAY: Why not?

LUCY: We've gone through it once. There's not any more room in the living room… We figured it out. We'll do it here…

DAVID: *(A pile of sheet music, over the end of this)* Rose, look at all this…

SALLY: *(To DAVID)* What's that?

ROSE: *(Surprised)* Sheet music…

DAVID: Remember that song we could never find? You wanted to make it into a dance—.

ROSE: *(Over this)* What song?

DAVID: Alice had told you about it. We could never find it.

SALLY: I know what you mean. Kate would be interested in this…

KATE: Why?

DAVID: Alice only ever knew its name. *(To LUCY who isn't listening)* The singer was a male impersonator, Lucy. And her theme song, its title: 'I've never seen a straight banana.'

(Laughter)

IRENIE: *(With a photo from the box)* Look what you wrote on the back, Rose. *(Reads)* 'Everything is possible if you'll just stand straight, get your weight on both feet and lift your—

IRENIE, SALLY & ROSE: — 'pelvis…'

ROSE: You can never say it enough. What's funny? Dancers, David…

DAVID: Do I know.

LUCY: We're ready. Whenever you are.

IRENIE: *(With a photo)* Maggie Black!

(Reaction from SALLY *and* ROSE*: 'Oh God.')*

MAY: Who's—?

ROSE: She was a fad. There were always fads.

IRENIE: She used to smoke as she danced. We'd all just watch the ash…

DAVID: That was Janet.

SALLY: You couldn't tell Viola that you were taking her class.

IRENIE: It was like high school.

SALLY: *(To the girls)* Dyed blond hair, big puffy thing sticking out of her head. Like out of 'What Happened to Baby ….'

IRENIE: You remember what Julie would say about her? Maggie. How she'd walk into her grave?

ROSE: What?

IRENIE: That she'd still be counting 5-6-7-and then 8 into the grave. And then, you'd hear: 'done.'

(Laughter)

ROSE: *(To* LUCY*)* You waiting on us? *(To* DAVID*, about* IRENIE *and* SALLY*)* These ladies are getting fresh… *(To the girls)* Where do you want me?

LUCY: We're mostly here.

ROSE: David, let's switch *(Chairs)*.

LUCY: Sally can you do the music…? It's all set. Just…

(Hands her the IPhone.)

IRENIE: This is the duet?

SALLY: The duet.

MAY: Keep that clear…

(The girls will get in position to make their entrance.)

SALLY: You need time to…?

LUCY: We just worked it out in the living room…

SALLY: Irenie, remember when Dwayne stopped and asked, 'what's the count?' And Rose just stared at him, and said, "it's at: 'And…'"

DAVID: They're waiting, Sally.

SALLY: *(To the girls)* Ready?

(LUCY and MAY nod.)

SALLY: And…

(Music: The Bowman Sisters' Old Lonesome Blues. The girls make their entrance and dance, after a short while:)

ROSE: Wait. Wait. Stop. Stop.

(They stop.)

ROSE: *(To SALLY)* Have you told them who they're dancing?

SALLY: I haven't. I was going to tell them later. We've just been working on the steps and the facings.

ROSE: You'll like this, May.

MAY: What??

ROSE: You're your mother.

MAY: What??? Wait… What?

LUCY: *(Over this)* I don't know anything about this.

ROSE: And Lucy, you're me. We're the tall sister. *(To KATE)* Kate, my sister never got over that. That I was taller. *(To SALLY)* You didn't tell them.

SALLY: I was going to.

ROSE: Kate, that's what this dance is about. Me and May's mother. As teenagers. Stuck in that moronic fucking motel that I keep warning you about, May.

And about the little competitions, you know, that are sometimes between sisters. Between my sister and me.

DAVID: That's an understatement.

MAY: *(To* LUCY*)* I'm my mother?

ROSE: You are. And Kate, she had this boyfriend…

MAY: What??

ROSE: He was going into the army. And he was a real jerk, May. In my humble opinion. You mother didn't agree, May. She had such bad taste in men. Still does. Anyway, years later, when I made the dance and my sister saw it, you should have seen how upset she got. *(Shrugs)* She has no sense of humor. None. That's because of Utica, May. Kate, sit with me.

(KATE *will sit next to* ROSE.)

SALLY: Again, girls?

(The girls move back to position.)

LUCY: *(To* MAY*)* Try not to think about it.

SALLY: Ready? And…

(Music. They dance.)

ROSE: Sassier. We were very sassy girls.

(They dance.)

ROSE: *(To* KATE*)* Two hick girls from Utica—bursting to get the hell out. Can you see that?

(They dance.)

SALLY: Nice.

(They dance.)

ROSE: Your Mom means business, May. She's showing off for that boyfriend.

(They dance.)

ROSE: *(To* IRENIE*)* That's a nice guy. *(Position)*

(ROSE *has become quiet, and as the dancers are finishing:*)

KATE: *(Standing)* Rose, you all right?

SALLY: Rose?

DAVID: *(Same time)* Rose... *(To* KATE*)* She all right?

SALLY: I don't know.

LUCY: *(Approaching* ROSE*)* Mom...?

IRENIE: Does she want some water?

KATE: Let her... Maybe you've danced enough for now.... Tired? Are you tired...? You want to lie down?

IRENIE: *(Over this)* What happened?

DAVID: I don't know...

LUCY: You all right, Mom?

IRENIE: She's tired, Lucy.

(ROSE *starts to get up.*)

ROSE: *(In pain)* Fuck....

KATE: Let's go upstairs. Your pills are upstairs in your bedroom...

LUCY: I can go get them.

KATE: We'll go up... Thanks. Thank you, Lucy.

(KATE *helps* ROSE *up.*)

KATE: We spent too long at the farmers' market. My fault. You had to look at everything... Take your time....

DAVID: *(To* ROSE*)* A very exciting day... The old gang together... Right, Rose?

KATE: Take it slow... I know....

(*As* MAY *tries to help:*)

KATE: Thank you, May...

(KATE *and* ROSE *go:*)

KATE: Dinner should be ready soon. Go ahead and serve yourselves...

(Pause)

IRENIE: I think you girls are doing great...

SALLY: *(To* LUCY *and* MAY*)* Hear that?

DAVID: *(To* LUCY*)* You all right? It is what it is...

IRENIE: *(To* MAY*)* So you had no idea you were your Mom...

MAY: No one told me...

(Pause)

DAVID: *(Again, to* LUCY*)* It is what is.

LUCY: I don't think I'm hungry. I'm going to go take a walk...

DAVID: Lucy...

MAY: I'll come with you...

(They pick up their shoes.)

LUCY: *(To* MAY*)* You want to drive somewhere? Or we can just take a walk down the driveway...

MAY: Whatever you want...

(They go. No one knows what to say.)

(Lights fade.)

8.
Practical Matters.

(The same, a short time later. DAVID *is taking out the quiche.)*

SALLY: David, you all right? *(Then)* 'It is what it is.'

DAVID: And what is that, Sally? *(Then)* The quiche looks good.

IRENIE: What's the soup?

SALLY: I think she said Provencal Lentil.

IRENIE: Sounds good.

SALLY: Irenie, could you clear that stuff away? Put it anywhere…David, I told Irenie that we've been thinking of finding someone to come up here and go through all the stuff with Rose….

DAVID: Be great.

SALLY: We've thought of tackling it ourselves…

IRENIE: You don't have the time.

DAVID: No.

SALLY: Ideally we'd get someone here asking Rose— what's this, who's that in that photo?

IRENIE: You said there's a lot more of this stuff in the living room?

SALLY: And the basement.

DAVID: They've started to rot… We've put in a dehumidifier. It runs all the time.

SALLY: We were talking about this in the car, and we came up with a crazy idea…

DAVID: What's the crazy idea?

SALLY: Of asking May…

DAVID: May?

IRENIE: She knows dance.

DAVID: To do what?

SALLY: To come up and sort through things. And live here with Rose for a while.

IRENIE: Go through all her stuff. May knows the names. And if she doesn't, I'm sure she knows how to find out who they are. Lucy's going to be away…I'd come up here and help but, you know, I work.

DAVID: Of course. Sally, May's not a nurse.

IRENIE: That's not what we're asking. Is it?

SALLY: *(Hesitates, then)* No. Of course not.

IRENIE: Kate doesn't know dance, David.

(They serve themselves:)

DAVID: May's Mom wants her to come back to Utica.

IRENIE: Right. She said that. *(A joke)* Hopefully not for too long. It's Utica.

SALLY: I heard her tell Lucy that her Mom's got some trouble with her knees and needs help with the motel. And she keeps saying to May, what the hell are you doing? All that studying to work at some stupid bar, live with three roommates? 'Come home. Come home.'

IRENIE: And is she going to go? Home? Do you think?

(SALLY *shrugs.*)

IRENIE: Is there somewhere up there in Utica where she can keep dancing? If not, that's a real shame… She's how old?

SALLY: I think twenty-four.

IRENIE: She can refuse to go. She has her own life… It sounds like her mom's just being clingy.

DAVID: She's her mom, Irenie.

IRENIE: And Rose is her mom's sister. She'd be helping out *her sister*. She'll understand that. The two of them, Rose and May, hanging out up here. It would be good for both of them. There's a lot to do up here now for May. It's not Utica. Bard. The Lumberyard in Catskill.

DAVID: You haven't even been.

IRENIE: I'm going to go. Kaatsbaan. You've become a center for dance. Who needs New York?

DAVID: Listen to yourself.

IRENIE: *(Over this)* How did that happen? And she and her aunt would have a lot to share…

DAVID: *(Again)* She's not a nurse.

IRENIE: *(Over this)* They share a history.

DAVID: What are you talking about?

IRENIE: Both left Utica. Both got the hell out of there to dance. The pull of both their mothers… That goddamn motel—.

(KATE *enters with a small notebook.*)

DAVID: Rose asleep?

KATE: No. Where are the girls?

SALLY: They're taking a walk.

KATE: They didn't want to eat?

DAVID: No.

IRENIE: Not yet.

SALLY: You think she'll come back down tonight?

KATE: I don't know.

IRENIE: I'm here for a week.

KATE: You find everything? You know there's soup.

IRENIE: I'm having some.

DAVID: You were up there a while.

KATE: She wanted to talk.

(Then)

DAVID: Want some wine?

IRENIE: *(Over this)* Kate, everything is great.

DAVID: *(To* KATE*)* Salad?

KATE: I will help myself... Rose just told me another of her amazing stories... That's why I was up there so...

IRENIE: She couldn't be that tired...

KATE: Another dance she still wants to do.

DAVID: She doesn't quit.

SALLY: Good for her.

DAVID: I agree.

IRENIE: What was the dance going to be about? Can you tell us or is it private?

KATE: *(As she serves herself)* It's not private, Irenie... Let me see... About some women who have been sentenced to what the gods believe will be eternal drudgery. Because of what they've done.

IRENIE: What have they done?

KATE: Killed their husbands.

SALLY: *(To* DAVID*)* Don't listen.

KATE: So sentenced now to endless mundane tasks. How's the quiche?

SALLY: Wonderful. Everything is, Kate.

KATE: The girls weren't hungry at all?

*(*SALLY *shrugs.)*

IRENIE: So they were sentenced...

KATE: To mundane tasks. Carrying a jug of water. Emptying it. Filling it up again, again and again. Doing laundry. Washing a floor, cooking... So the gods think they have punished these women to a kind of hell, but the women, in Rose's dance, as she just explained to me—the women will turn these mundane tasks into graceful, beautiful gestures... *(Then)* She said—and this I found interesting—there are certain parts of women's lives that have never ever been danced. From an old myth, I think.

IRENIE: She liked to do that.

SALLY: *(As a joke)* She's a terrible housekeeper, Rose.

IRENIE: On tour she never used a washing machine. Even if there was one in her apartment. I don't think she knows how…

KATE: She doesn't. *(Continues)* Praising housework. Drudgery. That's not very—P C. Is it?

IRENIE: *(Interested)* Did you say that to her?

KATE: She said, does that mean that it's not worth being danced?

(KATE *shrugs. They eat. Short pause*)

IRENIE: *(To* SALLY *and* DAVID*)* Maybe I shouldn't say this…

SALLY: Say what?

IRENIE: To Kate.

KATE: What, Irenie? Say it.

IRENIE: That we all know, she's a very clever woman, our Rose. We have experienced that. Haven't we? And so it does sound like—this dance she just told you about—maybe—. Is it her way of *(Searches for the word)* 'glorifying' all the help that she now needs? And all that you are doing for her, Kate? I just hope, Kate that you don't feel…

KATE: Feel what, Irenie?

IRENIE: Taken advantage of, I guess. By Rose.

KATE: What are you trying to say to me? Just say it.

IRENIE: You hardly knew Rose, and then you take on… Have all this just thrust on you. Shouldering all of this.

I see how you take care of her. It's wonderful to watch. *(To* SALLY*)* You see it every day, you said.

SALLY: I do. I know all she does for Rose.

KATE: She wants to move in with me. Into the village.

(IRENIE, SALLY *and* DAVID *are not surprised.*)

KATE: Oh. You all know that… She's already told you that… So she's talked about it with you. Anyway she finally asked me this morning at the farmer's market…

SALLY: And is that fair to you? What do you think?

IRENIE: Is this what you signed on for?

KATE: I didn't sign on for anything, Irenie. It's nothing about 'signing on…' *(Then)* This house. Her house— the bedrooms are upstairs. And even if you put a bed down here, the bathroom is up there… Mine has everything on one floor. No stairs—except to the cellar, and there's no reason she'd ever have to go down there. She's scared that Lucy will give up this trip… Feel she needs to stay and take care of 'her mother.' She just hates that.

DAVID: I know. We know.

KATE: She said we can rent a hospital bed. That's what she remembers Alice needing. I guess I'd put it in my bedroom.

SALLY: And you?

KATE: There's a couch in my study.

IRENIE: You live right in the village?

KATE: *(Nods)* It's small.

IRENIE: You'd only known each other for two months?

KATE: Yeh. *(Then)* And I wanted to run away. When she told me.

IRENIE: Sally said. God bless you, you didn't.

KATE: Not yet… *(She looks at* SALLY.*)*

SALLY: *(To* KATE*)* We haven't said anything to Irenie.

IRENIE: *(To* SALLY*)* About…?

KATE: I've told David and Sally. Lucy… And Rose. *(Then)* Irenie, I had a partner for a long time. We broke up about two years ago. I didn't want that. A couple of months ago, I get a letter from her, a long emotional letter; apologizing for things said; explaining how she'd been going through things that she's now figured out, and that she too is retired—which surprised me, she's younger—but she inherited some money—and she's rented a small house in the south of France of all places. And would I please join her. She'd happily pay for the plane ticket. She's written three more times. We've talked twice. Skyped twice.

SALLY: Kate's never been to France. Or even Europe. David, she told me this week that she did her college thesis on the French Revolution…

DAVID: Did you?

IRENIE: What are you going to do?

SALLY: *(To* IRENIE*)* They'd been together for years.

KATE: Some of it on and off.

SALLY: This woman has a child.

KATE: A son. I've been close to him. Pretty much helped raise him He's ten now. I'm missing him growing up… That clock's ticking. There's a lot more quiche. And the crepes.

SALLY: Quiche, crepes. French lentil soup. A French meal?

DAVID: Crossed my mind too.

KATE: *(Smiles)* Maybe. I didn't think of that... Maybe... *(To* IRENIE*)* Rose can sit out in my backyard. She loves it there.

SALLY: Kate has a wonderful garden.

DAVID: While it's still warm enough.

SALLY: She's a wonderful gardener. Why should we be surprised?

KATE: David, she now wants to make a garden in the park by the high school.

DAVID: Like the movie.

SALLY: Kate's garden's organized—. Tell her.

KATE: In three sections.

SALLY: No flowers...

IRENIE: What do you mean?

SALLY: *(Over this)* Japanese inspired.

IRENIE: What does that mean?

KATE: *(To* IRENIE, *explaining)* You walk down the drive and there's planting along the side. What's important is how wide this part of the path is. In fact, the whole journey is called 'the path.'

SALLY: She's done it beautifully.

KATE: Then you go through a gate.... And the path narrows, so you can only really walk in single file. The intention is to force one to have quiet conversations; because it's hard to talk in single file. Then through a second gate, and there's the stream—

DAVID: I haven't been.

SALLY: She's invited you.

KATE: *(Over this)* And here the path is all crooked and almost at random, so the hope, this is the theory, is to force people to look down, to watch where they walk.

And by looking down, we unconsciously, we look inward. 'Like with the best dances.'

IRENIE: What?

KATE: That's what Rose said when I took her through the first time… 'Like with the best dances. They try to help us look inward.'

IRENIE: Did she…

KATE: I see the books she's reading on her nightstand. She orders from library loan. She doesn't want to talk about *them*. I think she's embarrassed.

DAVID: What kind of books?

KATE: Spiritual stuff.

DAVID: That's not like her.

SALLY: *(To* KATE*)* I've seen them too. I've been surprised.

KATE: She saw me see her hiding them… I said, that is nothing to be embarrassed about… *(Smiles)*

IRENIE: What?

KATE: There's that wicker chair in her living room—and all of a sudden, for no reason, it makes creaking noises. Like someone very lightweight has sat down. She's shown me this. Pointed this out. She said—"Kate, listen for something like that. That will be me." *(Then)* She wants you all to see this.

(KATE *picks up the small notebook she brought from upstairs and hands it to* IRENIE:)

IRENIE: What's that? What's this…? *(She opens it. Looks through it.)* So she *is* facing things. Accepting. She's organizing her funeral, David.

KATE: It's back and forth. One day she'll just shut down if you mention it. Then another time she gets this notebook out and… Writes—which songs. Which dances. Which poems.

DAVID: She won't come down, but she wants to make sure we keep talking about her…

IRENIE: Look what she wants…

KATE: What??

IRENIE: "Sally to tell the shrink story."

SALLY: *(Surprised)* She wants that at her funeral??

KATE: She's just written that down. What is it?

DAVID: *(Over this)* I know this…

IRENIE: I've heard this.

SALLY: *(Over this)* Kate, the early days. There were just three of us, including her. And something happened, something didn't work out as planned; maybe someone had criticized her. I never knew. Anyway, she went into a deep depression.

DAVID: She did. Really bad…

SALLY: She wouldn't get out of bed. Days passed.

DAVID: Weeks.

SALLY: *(Over this)* Finally we went to her and said you have to get some help, Rose. See someone. A shrink. But she wouldn't until things got even worse and finally she says: I have an idea.

DAVID: Always had to be her idea.

IRENIE: Oh really?

SALLY: I should go to the shrink and she'd tell me what to say, as if I were the one feeling what she felt. And then I'd come back and tell her what words of wisdom the doctor had given me—her.

DAVID: It's true.

SALLY: *(Over this)* So I do this, and I come back and tell her, and she gets all upset, and says what the hell did I tell him that for, and how I had misstated what she was feeling—

(Laughter)

IRENIE: Rose...

SALLY: —which I hadn't—and how I had to go back and explain and 'this time get it right, Sally'. This went on for weeks and weeks, drove me crazy, but—she did get better... *(To* DAVID *and* IRENIE*)* I know why she wants me to tell that.

DAVID: Why do you think?

IRENIE: *(Same time)* Why?

SALLY: Because it's about how she always got other people to tell her stories.

(Pause)

KATE: Last week we visited the section of the cemetery across Mill Street. The newer part where 'Green Burials' take place. She said that is what she wants.

IRENIE: I don't know what that is.

DAVID: Organic... The coffin, everything. So after a time, there's nothing left. No trace. Just all back into the earth.

KATE: She was excited by this. Thought it was very 'progressive'. The right thing to do. Especially today. *(Smiles)*

SALLY: What's funny?

KATE: Then two or three days later, she's telling me what she wants on her headstone. I say, Rose if it's a green burial, there are no headstones. What are you talking about, she said. "I want a headstone!" *(Laughs. Then laughs again)*

SALLY: What else?

KATE: When she wanted me to rehearse a song for her funeral. She suddenly said—'wait, the alto part is what I could sing.' I said, Rose, I don't think you're going to be there… And she got that look, you know the look: 'how do you know?'

(Laughter)

DAVID: *(Now with the notebook)* She has a schedule for the day…

KATE: It's going to be a whole day. Her friends are to come together, sit, talk, cook together—she likes that idea. She's underlined it. Some dancing of course. And then eat together, and just talk about her. Tell stories about her. *(Then)* This is the song she wants me to sing. *(She sings:)*
Sweetly she sleeps my Alice fair,
Her cheek on the pillow pressed,
Sweetly she sleeps while her flaxen
Hair…
(Repeats:)
Sweetly she sleeps my Alice fair…
Are we finished? It looks like we're finished. We're not really hungry, are we?

IRENIE: No.

KATE: We hardly ate anything.

DAVID: Sorry.

KATE: I'm not hungry either.

SALLY: So we'll have plenty left over…

DAVID: For the girls.

IRENIE: And Rose. And I'm here all week.

DAVID: Midnight snacks.

KATE: I'll put some of this in the fridge. Keep it fresh.

SALLY: Let us help...

KATE: Let me do it. It's tiny in there. It's easier with one person... *(She goes off to the pantry.)*

SALLY: It's late...

DAVID: We'll eat it later.

IRENIE: She did a nice job.

SALLY: She did. I just wasn't hungry.

IRENIE: Me neither.

(ROSE enters in robe and barefoot.)

SALLY: Did we wake you?

ROSE: No. Where are the girls?

DAVID: Out for a walk. Sit down.

ROSE: And Kate?

(KATE is entering:)

KATE: I'm here. You want something to eat? You didn't have supper...

ROSE: No, no...

SALLY: A wonderful meal. Kate spoils us.

ROSE: She does that. Don't you?

KATE: I try.

SALLY: We've just finished... And it's getting late.

ROSE: Is it?

DAVID: *(To SALLY)* We haven't even made up Irenie's room.

IRENIE: I can do that.

DAVID: Kate, let us at least help with the dishes.

KATE: I'll do it. Just pile them up. I'll wash them... Please... *(To ROSE)* You all right? How are you feeling? Sit down.

(ROSE *sits.*)

DAVID: *(To* SALLY*)* We can stay another minute.

IRENIE: *(To say something)* Kate, so what was Lucy like as a student? I've been wanting to ask.

KATE: *(Shrugs)* It was the 9th grade.

IRENIE: *(To* ROSE*)* You must be exhausted.

ROSE: Me??

IRENIE: Entertaining us… Well I'm tired. I didn't get a lot of sleep last night.

ROSE: Why not?

IRENIE: I suppose I was excited about seeing you. *(With the notebook)* Kate was showing us this…

(ROSE *shrugs.*)

IRENIE: It's so peaceful here.

ROSE: It's the country, Irenie.

IRENIE: Ah. That's the reason.

ROSE: Where are the girls?

KATE: She wants a cigarette. She's going to look for May.

DAVID: They went for a walk.

ROSE: Maybe they're back…

KATE: Wear your jacket. It's on the hook. And put your boots on…

DAVID: *(To* ROSE*)* We'll come with you.

SALLY: I'll get your boots. *(She goes off to get the boots.)*

KATE: *(Calls)* The green rubber ones… By the back door. Irenie, I hope you get a good night's sleep in the country. And we'll see you all here in the morning for breakfast.

DAVID: *(Over this)* You don't have to… We can make breakfast.

KATE: I've planned it. Say no more. Fresh eggs from the farmers' market…

(Off, the 'dinner bell' is rung.)

DAVID: *(Explaining)* The girls must be scaring off the deer… The deer would just take over if you'd let them… *(To* ROSE*)* You say they'd come right into the house. And make themselves a cup of tea…

ROSE: I think they would. As soon as we're gone… *(She stands up.)* Last night I was sitting behind Lucy and May in the living room? They were talking. And I hear May say, 'you know, podcasts are like T V for your ears.' I had to lean over and say, 'or like radio.' *(Then)* I kept seeing ghosts, watching those girls dance.

IRENIE: Me too, me too.

DAVID: Kate, we're just here. Anything you need.

KATE: I know. I know.

(The bell is rung again.)

ROSE: The girls are back. May has cigarettes… *(She starts to go.)*

(SALLY *has returned with the boots.)*

SALLY: *(Holds up the boots)* Your boots, Rose.

KATE: Rose, wear your boots. Nice to meet you, Irenie…

IRENIE: And you, Kate. *(To* DAVID*)* She's barefoot, David.

DAVID: I've got your boots. Rose, wait… Will you wait?

(DAVID *follows* ROSE *off.)*

IRENIE: *(To* KATE*)* Goodnight. *(Follows:)* Jesus, put on your damn boots.

SALLY: *(To* KATE*)* See you in the morning.

KATE: I'll be here.

SALLY: 'Night.

KATE: Goodnight, Sally…

*(*SALLY *is gone.)*

*(*KATE *looks around at the mess.)*

(Music: Herzig's Best Day Of Our Lives.*)*

(She looks at a few napkins, then picks them all up and bunches them.)

(The bell is rung again off.)

(She tosses the napkins on the worktable. She will take a few dishes to the sink.)

(And KATE *begins to wash the dishes…)*

END OF PLAY

NOTE

In researching THE MICHAELS I consulted numerous books, archives, newspapers, etc. These are the most important books about dance: Sally Baines' three brilliant books: *Terpsichore in Sneakers, Democracy's Body: Judson Dance Theater,* and *Dancing Women: Female Bodies on Stage*; Yvonne Rainer's *Feelings Are Facts: A Life*; Twyla Tharp's *Push Comes To Shove: An Autobiography*; Paul Taylor's *Private Domain: An Autobiography*; Janice Ross' *Anna Halprin: Experience As Dance*; Connie Kreemer's *Further Steps: Fifteen Choreographers of Modern Dance; Merce Cunningham Dancing in Space and Time,* edited by Richard Kostelanetz; Marion Meyer's *Pina Bausch: The Biography; Europe Dancing,* edited by Andree Grau and Stephanie Jordon; *Dance: Documents of Contemporary Art,* edited by Andre Lepecki; *The Vision of Modern Dance,* edited by Jean Morrison Brown; C*ontemporary Dance: An Anthology of Lectures, Interviews and Essays,* edited by Anne Livet, Wendy Perron's *Through the Eyes of a Dancer.*

I am indebted to the Jerome Robbins Collection at the Performing Arts Library at Lincoln Center.

All of the dances credited to Rose Michael were in fact created in the 1970s and 80s by the great choreographer/dancer Dan Wagoner, and are used with his kind and generous permission.

THE MICHAELS is the first of a two-play series. This series is part of a group called *The Rhinebeck Panorama,* which also includes the four-play series, *The Apple Family,* a trilogy of Zoom plays about the Apple Family, and the three-play series, *The Gabriels.*

R.N.

www.ingramcontent.com/pod-product-compliance
Lightning Source LLC
Chambersburg PA
CBHW060203050426
42446CB00013B/2979